100

THINGS TO DO IN
SAN DIEGO
BEFORE YOU
DIE

Library of Congress Control Number: 2019952611

ISBN: 9781681062495

Design by Jill Halpin

All photos copyright David Swanson, except as noted.

Printed in the United States of America
20 21 22 23 24   5 4 3 2

We (the publisher and the author) have done our best to provide the most accurate information available when this book was completed. However, we make no warranty, guaranty, or promise about the accuracy, completeness, or currency of the information provided, and we expressly disclaim all warranties, express or implied. Please note that attractions, company names, addresses, websites, and phone numbers are subject to change or closure, and this is outside of our control. We are not responsible for any loss, damage, injury, or inconvenience that may occur due to the use of this book. When exploring new destinations, please do your homework before you go. You are responsible for your own safety and health when using this book.

100

2nd Edition

THINGS TO DO IN
SAN DIEGO
BEFORE YOU
DIE

● ●

DAVID SWANSON

REEDY PRESS

California Tower, Balboa Park

CONTENTS

Preface. x

Food and Drink

  1. Eat the Farm at A. R. Valentien. 2

  2. Add a Star to Your Dining Priorities with Addison 3

  3. Stake Your Claim at Born and Raised 4

  4. Kiss the High Tide at the Marine Room. 6

  5. Savor Mexico at Casa Guadalajara 7

  6. Splurge on a Grammy-Winner's Java at Bird Rock Coffee Roasters . . 8

  7. Loaf About at Bread & Cie 10

  8. Feast on Sumptuous Seafood at Ironside 11

  9. Slice Up a Mouth-Watering Craft Pizza at Il Dandy 12

10. Drink In the Sunset at Top of the Hyatt 14

11. Pick Sweet, Vine-Ripened Fruit at Carlsbad Strawberry Company . . . 15

12. Quaff Craft Suds at Stone Brewing World Bistro 16

13. Roll Up to the Bar for Omakase at Sushi Ota. 18

14. Revel in the Dramatic Bay and Skyline View at C Level 19

15. Satisfy Your Taco Cravings at ¡SALUD! 20

16. Indulge in Extraordinary Desserts. 22

17. Get Your Just Desserts with a Classic Julian Apple Pie 23

18. Go Local at the Hillcrest Farmers Market and Open-Air Bazaar 24

19. Raise the Bar on Craft Cocktails at Raised by Wolves 26

20. Cross the Border to Discover Mexico's Premiere Wine Region 27

21. Forage for Global Foods at Liberty Public Market 28

22. Dine on the Bay with Flagship Cruises 29

23. Mangia! Mangia! at Cucina Urbana 30

24. Celebrate the Local Suds during San Diego Beer Week 32

25. Evaluate Your Brunch Game at Morning Glory 33

26. Relish the Royale—with Cheese............................... 34

27. Devour an Asian Feast on Convoy Street 36

28. Quench Your Polynesian Fantasies with a Bali Hai Mai Tai......... 37

29. Reel in Fish Tacos for Lunch at Rubio's....................... 39

Music and Entertainment

30. Groove to Live Jams at Belly Up Tavern 42

31. Bend Your Ear for Summer Pops at San Diego Symphony's Shell ... 43

32. Purr with the Felines at San Diego Zoo 44

33. Roar and Snore with the Beasties of San Diego Zoo Safari Park 46

34. Enjoy Top Touring Acts at Humphrey's Concerts by the Bay 48

35. Don Your Best Drag for an Evening at Lips..................... 49

36. Rejoice in Christmas at the San Diego Parade of Lights 50

37. Flirt with Seadragons and Seahorses at Birch Aquarium 51

38. Take Me Out to a Padres Game at Petco Park 52

39. Rock at the Casbah.. 53

40. Meet a Sea Canary at SeaWorld 54

41. Seek Your Fortune in San Diego's Backcountry at a Casino Resort... 55

42. Kid Around at LEGOLAND................................. 56

• •

43. Dance the Night Away at Omnia. 58

44. Revel in the Adult Antics of Over-The-Line. 59

45. Sail Away to Distant Horizons from the Port of San Diego 60

46. Wander through the Flower Fields of Carlsbad 61

47. March for Independence Day and the Big Bay Boom. 62

Sports and Recreation

48. Honor the Undeveloped California Coastline at Torrey Pines. 66

49. Cycle the Bayshore Bikeway. 67

50. Rendezvous with Cetaceans on a Whale-Watching Tour 68

51. Dive Wreck Alley. 70

52. Look before You Leap into the Void at Torrey Pines Gliderport 71

53. Pamper Your Pooch at Dog Beach 72

54. Strip to Your Birthday Suit at Black's Beach. 73

55. Skate by the Sea at the Hotel del Coronado 74

56. Hike Mt. Woodson (and Take a Bite of Potato Chip Rock). 77

57. Sail the America's Cup Racing Yacht, *Stars & Stripes* 77

58. Run with the Grunions. 78

59. Muss Your Hair and Rattle Your Bones on the Giant Dipper. 79

60. Track Down a Deep-Fried Twinkie at the San Diego County Fair. . . . 80

61. Learn How to Ride the Waves with a Surf Diva 81

62. Amble along Sunset Cliffs for Dreamy Seaside Vistas 82

63. Paddle with Whales and Sea Lions and Sharks, Oh My! 85

64. Play One of America's Finest Golf Courses at Torrey Pines. 86

65. Lift Your Spirits with Spring Wildflowers in the
Anza-Borrego Desert. 88

• •

vii

66. Stroll the Oceanside Pier 89

67. Meander along Coastal Rocks and Discover the Tide Pools 90

68. Take Flight in a Hot Air Balloon. 92

69. Angle for a Bit on a Sportfishing Trip 94

70. Tackle the Five-Peak Challenge at Mission Trails 95

71. Navigate the Mission Beach Boardwalk. 96

Culture and History

72. Absorb the View at Cabrillo National Monument 100

73. Appreciate the Masterful Architecture of the Salk Institute 101

74. Explore the Museums of Balboa Park 102

75. Let the Waves Rock You to Sleep at Crystal Pier Hotel 104

76. Prowl the Legendary Hotel del Coronado 105

77. Commune with Pinnipeds at the Children's Pool. 106

78. Bring Your Passport to Taste the Real Tijuana with Turista Libre 108

79. Ferry to Beautiful Coronado Island 109

80. Find Your Zen in the Gardens of Balboa Park 111

81. Picture Art Alive at the San Diego Museum of Art. 112

82. Applaud the Bard at the Old Globe Theatre. 113

83. Daytrip to Palomar Observatory 114

84. Clamber Down to La Jolla's Sunny Jim Sea Cave 115

85. Rediscover American Naval History aboard USS *Midway* 117

86. Discover the Birthplace of San Diego in Old Town 118

87. Catch a Future Tony Winner at La Jolla Playhouse 119

88. Master Nautical History at the Maritime Museum of San Diego 121

89. Sketch Yourself into the Scene at Comic-Con 122

90. Pay Tribute to Mission Basilica San Diego de Alcalá 124

91. Picnic with a Free Outdoor Concert at the Spreckels
Organ Pavilion 126

92. Flock to the Living Coast Discovery Center 127

Shopping and Fashion

93. Browse with Tijuaneros at Las Americas Premium Outlets 130

94. Try On Your Designer Instincts along Cedros Avenue 132

95. Brush Shoulders with Famed Authors at Warwick's 133

96. Buy Original Art at Spanish Village Art Center 134

97. Surrender to Your Shopping Habit at Westfield UTC 135

98. Shop South of the Border without a Passport at Bazaar Del Mundo . . 136

99. Embark on a Retail Therapy Journey in Mission Valley 138

100. Lose Yourself in the Boutiques of La Jolla 140

Suggested Itineraries 141

Activities by Season 145

Index 146

PREFACE

As a third-generation San Diegan, I grew up living the quintessential California dream: beaches at my front door, lemon trees and rosemary bushes outside the pantry, and mountains and desert in my backyard. While I exaggerate—slightly—the proximity of these natural assets, there's no question that we are blessed with an outstanding location, and our benevolent Mediterranean climate allows San Diegans to embrace an outdoor lifestyle year-round.

I've watched the city evolve from the conservative surfer-and-sailor town of my childhood into a vibrant city with an economy that fires on all cylinders, as new tech and health industries find synergy with the established ones like education and defense. Over the last few decades, an influx of new talent has provided an infusion of new energy, ideas, and money to nourish cultural institutions, fuel our dining and nightlife, and stimulate older, run-down neighborhoods. Today, we celebrate a well-funded San Diego Symphony (California's oldest), a San Diego restaurant that earned the coveted Michelin star (Addison), and neighborhoods such as South Park and Barrio Logan that have become enticing draws for locals and visitors alike.

Humming in the background is tourism, a lifeblood for the city. I've been writing about travel to San Diego since 1995 and writing this book has reminded me of activities I hadn't explored in years. But it also introduced me to new discoveries I was excited to find—and to share now with you. In narrowing the list to a nice, round hundred, I strived for a geographical spread that kept a focus on neighborhoods

• •

in the core city but included a handful of recommendations that lie at the edges of San Diego County—forty, fifty, or more miles from downtown. And although there are certainly splurge experiences to be treasured (hot air balloon ride, anyone?), you'll find lots of free or gently priced activities and meals celebrated in these pages.

As always, the assistance of the knowledgeable team at the San Diego Tourism Authority—Robert, Joe, Sarah, and Edna—provided suggestions and fact-checking help at crucial points. My immediate San Diego family—Anthony, Sarah, Erik, Denise, Hayley, and Chanelle—offered input that helped me narrow the list at several points, whether they knew it or not. And Chris kept the home fires burning—always supportive, always organized, always loving. Thank you, all.

Now, pack a laid-back attitude along with your sandals and swimsuit (and a sweater for those cool summer evenings!), and let's uncover the best of California's grown-up beach town.

Pizzeria Buona Forchetta

FOOD AND DRINK

EAT THE FARM
AT A. R. VALENTIEN

While "farm to table" has emerged as a go-to trend in the early 2000s, few cities in the US could better support such sensible cooking than San Diego, where year-round farms dot the backcountry, providing a wide variety of produce within an hour or two of the cutting board. Executive Chef Jeff Jackson's market-inspired menu at A. R. Valentien is dictated by the season. Classic dishes like chicken liver pâté, duck confit, a twenty-eight-day dry-aged prime rib eye steak, or vermouth-braised sea bass share the plate with such delicacies as preserved Meyer lemons, pickled carrots, Chioggia beets, morel mushrooms—all tasting more rich and ambrosial than we mortals have any right to expect. The setting is the handsome and gracious Lodge at Torrey Pines, a Craftsman-style golf resort, in a room adorned with stained glass, metal-wrapped wood beams, and *plein-air* paintings of Southern California landscapes.

11480 N. Torrey Pines Rd., 858-777-6635
lodgetorreypines.com/ar-valentien
Neighborhood: Torrey Pines

ADD A STAR TO YOUR DINING PRIORITIES
WITH ADDISON

San Diego chefs have long lamented the lack of respect for their restaurant scene on the national stage. Critics appear to be making up for this lamentable oversight because in 2019, Addison was the city's first restaurant to be recognized with a star from Michelin, the world's oldest restaurant guide. Sitting amid the sumptuous grounds of the Fairmont Grand Del Mar resort, the kitchen is under the direction of Executive Chef William Bradley, a four-time James Beard Award nominee who cites Thomas Keller as one of his mentors. Count on twenty-two-karat gold trimmings, fireplaces, formal ambience, doting service, and unstinting contemporary French cuisine interpreting such luxury items as Alaskan king crab, Kaluga Queen caviar, veal sweetbreads, and barbecued pigeon in creative yet unpretentious ways. Choose either the five- or ten-course tasting menu ($175 and $275, respectively) for a meal that brings food critics to their knees.

5200 Grand Del Mar Way, 858-314-1900
addisondelmar.com
Neighborhood: Carmel Valley

STAKE YOUR CLAIM
AT BORN AND RAISED

When Born and Raised opened in the space of a beloved Little Italy camera shop, one could say the bar for steakhouses across the city was raised. The restaurant, possibly San Diego's most costly, sells dueling experiences: swank Great Gatsby styling downstairs with sumptuous brass finishings and voluptuous beaded woodwork versus the upstairs hip, open-air, casual vibe on a teak terrace, tinged with frat-boy irreverence. No matter: you came for the steaks, and with a glassed-in dry-aging room and butcher shop, you'll want to invest heartily in a swaggering bone-in ribeye or T-bone. The decadent tableside preparations range from frosty Manhattans to fiery Caesars, from voluptuous Tournedos Rossini to simple ice cream hand-cranked on a tricked-out, gold-plated mixer. It all adds up to a very special evening out.

1909 India St. 619-202-4577

bornandraisedsteak.com

Neighborhood: Little Italy

OTHER STEAKHOUSE FAVORITES

Cowboy Star Restaurant and Butcher Shop
Western-inspired, contemporary and sophisticated.

640 Tenth Ave., 619-450-5880
cowboystar.com
Neighborhood: Downtown

Rare Society
Vegas styling in a cozy neighborhood joint.

4130 Park Blvd., 619-501-6404
raresocietysd.com
Neighborhood: University Heights

Island Prime
Steaks with a view, in a swank setting

880 Harbor Island Dr., 619-298-6802
cohnrestaurants.com/islandprime
Neighborhood: Harbor Island

Turf Supper Club
Grill your own at retro neighborhood pick; open late.

1116 Twenty-Fifth St., 619-234-6363
turfsupperclub.com
Neighborhood: Golden Hill

Bully's East Prime Bistro Sports Bar
Old-school sports bar and local favorite for prime rib.

2401 Camino del Rio S., 619-291-2665
bullyseastsd.com
Neighborhood: Mission Valley

KISS THE HIGH TIDE
AT THE MARINE ROOM

A San Diego icon since 1941, the Marine Room sits at the shore's edge, a barely-legal position today. Most evenings, tides roll across the sand lazily, the water barely lapping at the building. But during unusually high summer tides, dinner beside the restaurant's wall-to-wall windows can be quite a thrill, with waves crashing against the glass between every bite. Fortunately, the food, a decadent (and *trés cher*) marriage of French and Asian under the watch of Executive Chef Bernard Guillas, lives up to the spectacle, with such favorites as sesame-spiced ahi tuna and Thai-style butter-basted lobster tail emphasizing an ocean-to-table aesthetic. Ideally, you might schedule your reservation for an hour or so before high tide—if you're lucky, it will coincide with sunset—to enjoy the scampering sandpipers and fishing pelicans before the parade of illuminated rollers arrives to splash your view.

2000 Spindrift Dr., 858-459-7222
marineroom.com
Neighborhood: La Jolla Shores

SAVOR MEXICO
AT CASA GUADALAJARA

One cuisine tops the list for most San Diego visitors: Mexican. While there are dozens of decent Mexican restaurants and hundreds of taco shops throughout the city, identifying one standout that consistently delivers delicious food, a menu with a wide variety of options (including vegetarian), and a festive, memorable ambience is easy. Sitting comfortably at the front of the line is Casa Guadalajara. The restaurant has an inviting outdoor patio with burbling fountains under a giant pepper tree, or you may choose to dine indoors with the piñatas. Either way, you'll be serenaded by mariachis as you sample traditional and regional Mexican specialties, such as cochinita pibil—Yucatan pork baked in achiote and orange juice with pickled red onions and yellow chiles. Food portions are copious, the margaritas are birdbath-size, and the waitresses are decked out in ruffled folkloric dresses.

4105 Taylor St., 619-295-5111
casaguadalajara.com
Neighborhood: Old Town

SPLURGE ON A GRAMMY-WINNER'S JAVA
AT BIRD ROCK COFFEE ROASTERS

Blue Mountain Coffee from Jamaica is a pricey pour, and the farms of Kona, Hawaii produce excellent coffee that can cost a pretty penny. But the world's most expensive coffee is a low-yield varietal called Geisha, and, freshly roasted, it can run $100 a pound and up—when you can find it. Rarer still is the Geisha varietal grown and harvested on a farm in San Diego by none other than singer Jason Mraz. First offered in 2019, a cup costs $35, and a four-ounce bag sells for $199. The Grammy-winner's coffee, along with considerably less expensive options, can be enjoyed—when in stock—exclusively at Bird Rock Coffee Roasters, where the pour-over is a careful performance involving 200-degree water delicately poured over precisely ground beans in timed pulses into a glass carafe.

5627 La Jolla Blvd., 760-269-8609
birdrockcoffee.com
Neighborhood: La Jolla

2212 Carmel Valley Rd.
760-269-8799
Neighborhood: Torrey Pines

2295 Kettner Blvd., 760-269-8938
Neighborhood: Little Italy

829 Garnet Ave., 858-634-9115
Neighborhood: Pacific Beach

1270 Morena Blvd., 760-269-8618
Neighborhood: Morena

OTHER FINE COFFEE ROASTERS
WORTH DISCOVERING

Dark Horse Coffee Roasters

3260 Adams Ave., Normal Heights, 619-344-6962
3794 Thirtieth St., North Park, 619-955-7447
811 Twenty-Fifth St., Golden Hill, 619-344-0500
4350 Palm Ave. #104, La Mesa, 619-344-0550
darkhorsecoffeeroasters.com

Caffè Calabria

3933 Thirtieth St., North Park, 619-683-7787
caffecalabria.com

WestBean Coffee Roasters

240 Broadway, Downtown
2820 Historic Decatur Rd., Point Loma
2550 Fifth Ave. #75, Hillcrest
4140 Morena Blvd., Bay Ho
thewestbean.com

Mostra Coffee

12045 Carmel Mtn. Rd. #302
Carmel Mountain Ranch, 858-304-0061
mostracoffee.com

LOAF ABOUT
AT BREAD & CIE

The scent of baking bread permeates this beloved Hillcrest bakery and café, where artisanal European bread-making is practiced daily. Every loaf is made with natural ingredients, organic flour, and natural starters for leavening, with careful attention paid to the fine points of texture and crust. The result is bread that is served at dozens of the city's best restaurants. More than two dozen kinds of bread are on the roster daily, while some of them (like the deliciously meaty walnut and scallion) pop up just once or twice a week. The work of local artists, changed monthly, adorns the walls of Bread & Cie, to the delight of the bakery's decidedly European clientele. Even if you are not a baguette booster, you can still enjoy the bakery's house-made granola, elegant tarts, and scones for breakfast, or the Mediterranean-inspired soups and sandwiches at lunch.

350 University Ave., 619-683-9322
breadandcie.com
Neighborhood: Hillcrest

FEAST ON SUMPTUOUS SEAFOOD
AT IRONSIDE

Little Italy has been known for Italian restaurants (natch!) as long as anyone can recall, but there was precious little to showcase the neighborhood's true heritage—that of the fishermen who worked San Diego's tuna fleet into the 1970s. Ironside has taken care of that in a polished warehouse setting embellished with humorous seafaring touches, like one tentacle-shaped light fixture and a wall littered with piranha heads. The menu changes daily with the fresh, local catch (the fishermen are cited), but outstanding dishes include the sloppy, decadent lobster roll dressed in brown butter mayo; clam chowder awash in hearty bacon; and an octopus tentacle in a sauce of olives, chorizo, and sherry. Or go for broke with the $420 platter loaded with white sturgeon caviar, ceviche, two pounds of Maine lobster, and more. Too rich for your blood? The don't-miss weekday happy hour rewards the frugal with one-dollar blue point oysters, tacos, and gumbo.

1654 India St., 619-269-3033
ironsidefishandoyster.com
Neighborhood: Little Italy

SLICE UP A MOUTH-WATERING CRAFT PIZZA
AT IL DANDY

In 2013, Tripadvisor named San Diego America's number one city for pizza. While New Yorkers scoffed, San Diegans, well . . . kept eating craft pizzas, content to keep the Neapolitan creativity flowing. Il Dandy may be nothing like your neighborhood pizza joint, but the inspired gastronomy of Michelin-starred Calabrian chef Antonio Abbruzzino inspires what is probably the city's finest (and priciest) pizza. The dough is made from three flours and fermented for three days before baking, creating a lighter-than-air crust. Toppings include pumpkin, *guanciale*, truffle, hazelnut, and pecorino for the *Buongustaia* pizza; or codfish, escarole, olive, mozzarella, and raisins for the *Mammolese*. But don't stop with pies: other dishes that dazzle include ravishing pastas along with exquisite calamari, branzino, smoked lamb, and dry-aged ribeye, all served in a chic, airy space filled with glass and modern art. Il Dandy is clearly not your grandfather's pizzeria.

2550 Fifth Ave., 619-310-5669
ildandyrestaurant.com
Neighborhood: Bankers Hill

OTHER SPOTS FOR TASTY CRAFT PIZZA

Buona Forchetta

3001 Beech St., South Park, 619-381-4844
2865 Sims Rd., Liberty Station, 619-548-5770
buonaforchettasd.com

Ambrogio15

926 Turquoise St., Pacific Beach, 858-291-8650
ambrogio15.com

Pummarò Pizzeria

1101 Scott St., Point Loma, 619-224-2272
pummaropizzeria.com

Siamo Napoli

3959 Thirtieth St., North Park, 619-310-6981
siamonapolisd.com

Tribute Pizza

3077 North Park Way, North Park, 619-450-4505
tributepizza.com

Bronx Pizza
(takeout and delivery only)

111 Washington St., Hillcrest, 619-291-3341
bronxpizza.com

DRINK IN THE SUNSET
AT TOP OF THE HYATT

San Diego's ultimate sky lounge occupies the fortieth floor of the West Coast's tallest waterfront building, the Manchester Grand Hyatt. Through floor-to-ceiling windows, Top of the Hyatt offers a near-360-degree view of the burgeoning downtown skyline, Coronado, the San Diego Bay marinas and harbor, and the Naval Air Station North Island, where aircraft carriers are berthed. On clear days you'll see Tijuana on the horizon. While the bar's décor is a bit austere, the view at sunset is unrivaled, and the bartender mixes a mean Campfire Old Fashioned. The drinks aren't cheap, but the selection of appetizers and desserts is inviting, plus parking is validated for three hours—no small consideration downtown.

1 Market Pl., 619-232-1234
topofthehyatt.com
Neighborhood: Downtown

TIP
Altitude Sky Lounge is a twenty-second-floor alternative, perched atop the Marriott Gaslamp Quarter and looking straight down on the Padres' Petco Park. There's a nightly happy hour (5:00 to 7:00) and DJs spinning on select nights (660 K St., 619-446-6086, altitudeskylounge.com).

PICK SWEET, VINE-RIPENED FRUIT
AT CARLSBAD STRAWBERRY COMPANY

San Diego County is one of the nation's most important farm economies—it has more small farms than any other county, and it's among the top producers of avocados, lemons, and tomatoes. We're also in the top ten for strawberries, and the Carlsbad Strawberry Company's forty-acre farm has been growing the berries for four generations in a field situated between Interstate 5 and the Batiquitos Lagoon. Strawberries are the first fruit to ripen in the spring, so the harvest usually starts in January. Better yet, pick your own starting in February or March (once the fields are less muddy), and continue to do so through early July. The county's temperate climate and abundant sunshine make for deliciously sweet strawberries, so take your time while walking through the fields to look for the ripest ones. Remember, those buckets fill up fast!

1050 Cannon Rd., 760-603-9608
carlsbadstrawberrycompany.com
Neighborhood: Carlsbad

QUAFF CRAFT SUDS
AT STONE BREWING WORLD BISTRO

San Diego's beloved beer giant Stone Brewing—ninth-largest craft brewery in the US—is also noted for two restaurants serving creative pub fare in handsomely designed settings. The globe-girdling menu ranges from wok-fried cauliflower spiked with Szechuan peppers, chicken schnitzel, andouille sausage and kale bucatini, Moroccan spiced hanger steak, burgers, tacos, and entrée-size salads. A draft list of over forty beers includes special-release Stone beers not available elsewhere, along with a rotating selection from other fine breweries. The six-hundred-seat venue at Liberty Station in Point Loma sprawls into a garden with waterways, a bocce ball court, and an outdoor cinema. Be aware that the restaurant lies right in the airport's flight path—a sure conversation stopper—but indoor seating is also available. At the Escondido location, forty-five minutes north of downtown, you can visit the original brewery before dining, with tours available from noon to 6:00 p.m. daily.

2816 Historic Decatur Rd., Point Loma, 619-269-2100
1999 Citracado Parkway, Escondido, 760-294-7866
stonebrewing.com/visit/bistros

OTHER GREAT BREWPUBS
FOR CRAFT BEER LOVERS

Blind Lady Ale House (Automatic Brewing)

3416 Adams Ave., Normal Heights, 619-255-2491
automaticbrewingco.com

Ballast Point

2215 India St., Little Italy, 619-255-7213
ballastpoint.com

Coronado Brewing

170 Orange Ave., Coronado, 619-437-4452
coronadobrewing.com

Alpine Beer Company Pub

1347 Tavern Rd., Alpine, 619-445-2337
alpinebrewing.com

Pizza Port

1956 Bacon St., Ocean Beach, 619-224-4700
135 N. Highway 101, Solana Beach, 858-481-7332
571 Carlsbad Village Dr., Carlsbad, 760-720-7007
pizzaport.com

Karl Strauss Brewing Co.

1157 Columbia St., Downtown, 619-234-2739
1044 Wall St., La Jolla, 858-551-2739
9675 Scranton Rd., Sorrento Mesa, 858-587-2739
5801 Armada Dr., Carlsbad, 760-431-2739
karlstrauss.com

ROLL UP TO THE BAR FOR OMAKASE
AT SUSHI OTA

Since 1990, Yukito Ota has been serving San Diego's finest sushi in a proudly unassuming strip mall next to the Interstate 5. While the 7-Eleven façade may lack glamor, inside you'll find understated chic. Chef Ota's offerings are also sophisticated, drawing the adventurous for an *omakase* (tasting) menu that always stars the locally sourced *uni* (sea urchin). Ota says his is the best he's ever tasted, served in nigiri form over rice. You can find American-style sushi rolls, but aficionados steer to the more traditional Japanese sushi and sashimi, all lightly garnished. I recommend the *ankimo* (monkfish liver) which is revered in Japan; *chawanmushi*, a delicate egg custard; and locally caught *amaebi*, live sweet shrimp prepared as nigiri or sashimi. Or take your cues from the warm, welcoming staff, especially if seated at the bar where chefs may deliver something unexpected. Reservations are strongly advised.

4529 Mission Bay Dr., 858-270-5670
sushiota.com
Neighborhood: Pacific Beach

REVEL IN THE DRAMATIC BAY AND SKYLINE VIEW
AT C LEVEL

No restaurant offers a better perch for taking in the San Diego Bay and downtown skyline panorama than C Level—full stop. Located on Harbor Island, a manmade peninsula close to the San Diego Airport, C Level manages to usher newcomers right into the San Diego spirit, which is why it's a favorite of mine for introducing visitors to the city. A seat on the outdoor terrace rewards the traveler with front-row views of passing cruise and navy vessels. The California-Med menu is not meant to impress foodies, but winning dishes include Hawaiian ahi and salmon poke and the crab Louie salad. Skirts on Fire comprises a spicy skirt steak and blue cheese atop a tasty salad. While C Level can be packed at sunset, especially for the weekday happy hour, it's also a great spot for lunch.

880 Harbor Island Dr., 619-298-6802, cohnrestaurants.com/islandprime
Neighborhood: Harbor Island

TIP
The adjacent Island Prime steakhouse and high-end Cali-Baja restaurant Coasterra—overseen by C Level's management—offer essentially the same CinemaScope view, but I have a slight preference for the unimpeded vista from C Level.

SATISFY YOUR TACO CRAVINGS
AT ¡SALUD!

San Diego and Tijuana are joined at the hip, so it only makes sense that our neighbor's favorite food is omnipresent and cherished everywhere, from food trucks to corner taco shops and from Mexican restaurants to luxe gourmet eateries. Somewhere in between is ¡SALUD!, a casual eatery in Barrio Logan, hub of Latin pride and culture. The Tijuanan-style street tacos, crafted with handmade tortillas, include traditional favorites like juicy carnitas with avocado or *pollo asado* stuffed with mesquite-grilled chicken and lathered in guacamole. Stretch your taste buds on the *taco de barrio* with beef, nopal cactus, beans, and sour cream or a side of fire-roasted corn with lime, *queso fresca*, *crema*, and chile. ¡SALUD! posts a solid list of draft beers, and the busy taqueria is done up with tattoo-inspired murals and a gleaming car hood, while outside the low riders, shiny bikes, and skate boarders congregate.

2196 Logan Ave., 619-255-3856, saludtacos.com
Neighborhood: Barrio Logan

MORE PLACES TO ENJOY CALI-BAJA TACOS

Cantina Mayahuel

2934 Adams Ave., North Park, 619-283-6292
facebook.com/cantinamayahuel

Las Cuatro Milpas (lunch only)

1875 Logan Ave., Barrio Logan, 619-234-4460
facebook.com/Las-Cuatro-Milpas-421776945082

Puesto

789 W. Harbor Dr., Downtown, 619-233-8880
1026 Wall St., La Jolla, 858-454-1260

City Tacos

3028 University Ave., North Park, 619-296-2303
8325 La Mesa Blvd., La Mesa, 619-467-7999
805 Ocean Lane, Imperial Beach, 619-621-5814
4516 Mission Blvd., Pacific Beach
citytacossd.com

Galaxy Taco

2259 Avenida De La Playa, La Jolla Shores, 858-228-5655
galaxytaco.com

TIP

Throughout San Diego, Taco Tuesday is honored like a religious
holiday, even at restaurants not focused on south-of-the-border
menus. Anticipate taco deals and at Old Town's Mexican venues,
expect crowds.

INDULGE IN EXTRAORDINARY DESSERTS

Truth in advertising: the desserts at this cherished institution are to die for (though not before you check off the other ninety-nine things cited in this book!). Pastry chef Karen Krasne has been satisfying San Diego's sweet tooth since 1988, as well as our cravings for butter cream, Valrhona chocolate, and ornamentation of fruit, rose petals, and gold leaf. Krasne, who has trained with French masters at Cordon Bleu, Lenôtre, and Pierre Hermé, specializes in decadent cakes—sold whole or by the generous slice—as well as scones, tarts, brownies, Napoleons, and—well, the list goes on—many of them marked by unusual flavor combinations. Both locations offer satisfying savory menus, including paninis, grilled cheese, soups, salads, and delicious charcuterie and cheese plates. The tea and coffee are nicely chosen, and beer and wine are also on offer.

2870 Fourth Ave., Bankers Hill, 619-294-2132
1430 Union St., Little Italy, 619-294-7001
extraordinarydesserts.com

GET YOUR
JUST DESSERTS
WITH A CLASSIC JULIAN APPLE PIE

The Julian Pie Company, founded in 1986, got its start when Liz Smothers was peeling apples and baking pies for a local pie shop. As more people sought out her pie-making services, Smothers decided to start her own business in Julian, a mountain community of about 1,500 residents. With apples and other fruit coming from local orchards, the pies became renowned for their flaky golden crust, and today are shipped around the country. Among more than twenty different types, the number-one seller is Dutch apple, with other favorites being apple mountain berry crumb, pecan, and strawberry-rhubarb. Sugar free pies are also available. The mountain town is a delight to discover, but if you don't want to make the trek to Julian—a ninety-minute drive from downtown—a number of San Diego grocers sell fresh Julian Pies, including most Vons supermarkets.

2225 Main St., 760-765-2449
julianpie.com
Neighborhood: Julian

GO LOCAL
AT THE HILLCREST FARMERS MARKET AND OPEN-AIR BAZAAR

Harboring more small farms than any other county in the nation, San Diego has access to a bounty of fresh produce year-round, and on any day of the week there are several farmers markets to be found where you can sample the produce of regional farmers and purchase treats or craft items from local artisans. The Sunday Hillcrest Farmers Market is the largest, drawing more than 10,000 people weekly who peruse the wares of about 175 vendors selling a wide variety of local produce and bread, cheese, olive oils, and meats. You'll find flowers and clothing, and at the south end of the street, the "food court" offers a bounty of international cuisine, from ceviche to African-spiced grilled food, and from Korean barbecue to Vietnamese coffees.

3960 Normal St., 619-237-1632
hillcrestfarmersmarket.com
Neighborhood: Hillcrest

TIP
Another good option for a Sunday farmers market is La Jolla's, held from 9:00 a.m. to 1:30 p.m. at 7335 Girard Avenue. All proceeds benefit La Jolla Elementary School: lajollamarket.com.

OTHER SAN DIEGO FARMERS MARKETS TO VISIT

Monday: Escondido
3:00 p.m. to 7:00 p.m.
8860 Lawrence Welk Dr.

Tuesday: Coronado
2:30 p.m. to 6:00 p.m.
1201 First St. (Ferry Landing)

Wednesday: Ocean Beach
4:00 p.m. to 7:00 p.m.
4900 block of Newport, between Cable and Bacon

Thursday: North Park
3:00 p.m. to 7:30 p.m.
2900 North Park Way

Friday: Imperial Beach
2:00 p.m. to 6:00 p.m.
10 Evergreen Ave.

Saturday: Little Italy
8:00 a.m. to 2:00 p.m.
West Cedar St. from Kettner to Front St.

RAISE THE BAR ON CRAFT COCKTAILS
AT RAISED BY WOLVES

A suburban mall is not where you'd normally look for the most unusual bar in the city, and yet that is where you'll find Raised by Wolves, cleverly hidden along a nondescript passageway at Westfield UTC. By day, it's a bottle shop, but one look at the curated selection of rare spirits posing behind polished glass and you'll know this is no ordinary liquor store. By evening—4:00 p.m. to be exact—the boutique's fireplace becomes a secret passageway into an ornate speakeasy-style bar. In decor, it's part French Art Nouveau and part Art Deco, with a healthy dash of Disney staging to set jaws agape. Beneath the domed stained-glass ceiling sits a circular bar with an ornate water fountain at its center, where bartenders mix riffs on a litany of classic cocktails, creating unexpected, often ambrosial, elixirs. Make a reservation and prepare to be delighted.

4545 La Jolla Village Dr., 619-629-0243
raisedxwolves.com
Neighborhood: La Jolla

CROSS THE BORDER
TO DISCOVER MEXICO'S PREMIERE WINE REGION

While California wineries are treasured for their quality and abundance, it was Mexico that produced the first wine in the Americas, using grapevines brought over by the Spanish in the sixteenth century. The humid winters and dry warm summers of Northern Baja allow for most of the same varietals produced in California, and Guadalupe Valley, northeast of Ensenada, is just ninety minutes from the San Diego-Tijuana border. Here, wines of surprising quality can be enjoyed—they're rarely exported north of the border. While driving down to Guadalupe Valley isn't hard, after considering insurance, border crossing, and designated drivers, you may want to leave the driving to someone else. Baja Winery Tours offers group tours weekly and private or overnight trips on request. You'll visit two different wineries for eye-opening tastings and enjoy a four-course gourmet lunch at a fine restaurant. Passport required.

Baja Winery Tours, 619-535-9994, bajawinerytours.com

TIP
Temecula, one of Southern California's major wine-producing regions, is just an hour north of San Diego. There are more than forty wineries in Temecula Wine Country, and many have tasting rooms and restaurants as well as gift shops. temeculawines.org

FORAGE FOR GLOBAL FOODS
AT LIBERTY PUBLIC MARKET

Who would have thought a decade ago that Liberty Station, the former Naval Training Center, would become one of San Diego's favorite places to hang out? In addition to restaurants, a movie theatre, arts district, and even an outdoor ice-skating rink at New Year's, Liberty Public Market is the biggest draw, with more than thirty vendors offering a range of cuisines from quick-service counters. Try Cane Patch Kitchen for jambalaya, seafood gumbo, and po'boys, or visit Bao Bar for Chinese buns and boba tea. At Latin Chef look for Peruvian ceviche and beef heart kebabs, or step up to Olala, where savory and sweet crepes are prepared using organic buckwheat flour imported from Brittany. There's also locally procured seafood, an old-fashioned butcher, a bottle shop, and much more. Go for live music on Sunday afternoons or the happy hour on weekdays from 3:00 to 6:00 p.m.

2820 Historic Decatur Rd., 619-487-9346
bluebridgehospitality.com/libertypublicmarket
Neighborhood: Point Loma

DINE ON THE BAY
WITH FLAGSHIP CRUISES

A dinner cruise across San Diego Bay reveals this great natural harbor's finest assets: views of the downtown skyline, Coronado Island, Naval Air Station North Island, and the shipyards along the city's working waterfront. Enjoy the bay in comfort aboard a Flagship cruise for a sunset or nighttime journey with a family-owned operator that has been sailing the bay since 1915. The three-course dinner prepared onboard is served several ways, ranging from an elegant prime rib dinner on Sundays to the more laid-back Friday Hops on the Harbor cruise which includes a flight of beer from local breweries. While it may not be the peak of gourmet dining, Flagship's seafood is sustainably sourced and most of the produce is local, so tip back a glass of sparkling wine and marvel at the twinkle of city lights as you float beneath the Coronado Bridge.

990 N. Harbor Dr., 619-234-4111
flagshipsd.com
Neighborhood: Downtown

MANGIA! MANGIA!
AT CUCINA URBANA

San Diego is full of solid Italian restaurants, especially in very busy Little Italy, but it's the wildly popular Cucina Urbana, Tracy Borkum's celebration of hearty, farm-style fare that rises as my favorite. The large venue is creatively furnished with custom and reclaimed elements, such as odd light fixtures and vintage Italian movie posters. It's like a rustic farmhouse with an artistic bent. The menu evolves seasonally, but staples include a velvety chicken liver pâté served with wine-soaked figs, fried squash blossoms stuffed with lemon ricotta, and creamy mascarpone polenta boards, ladled with the chef's daily ragu whim. There are creative Neapolitan pizzas and robust pastas garnished with California inspiration and served family style, and the half chicken fra diavolo will knock your socks off. Grab a bottle in the wine shop and take advantage of the modest corkage fee. It's wise to make reservations well ahead.

505 Laurel St., 619-239-2222
urbankitchengroup.com/cucina-urbana-bankers-hill/
Neighborhood: Bankers Hill

MORE ITALIAN RESTAURANTS WORTH DISCOVERING

Il Dandy
2550 Fifth Ave., Bankers Hill, 619-310-5669
ildandyrestaurant.com

Siamo Napoli
3959 Thirtieth St., North Park, 619-310-6981
siamonapolisd.com

Piacere Mio
1947 Fern St., South Park, 619-794-2543
piaceremiosd.com

Civico 1845
1845 India St., Little Italy, 619-431-5990
civico1845.com

Biga
950 Sixth Ave. C, Downtown, 619-794-0444
bigasandiego.com

CELEBRATE THE LOCAL SUDS
DURING SAN DIEGO BEER WEEK

Serving as a frothy closeout to the long summer, the region's bounteous beer culture is toasted in early November during San Diego Beer Week. The ten-day—who's counting?—county-wide festival is sponsored by the local brewer's guild. The region's local craft beers, brewed by more than 150 county breweries, have been collecting serious accolades at competitions around the world. It's a cozy scene—the brewers even collaborate on a Capital of Craft IPA to showcase San Diego's favorite beer style. Today, with craft beer contributing $850 million in annual revenue to the county, Beer Week encompasses more than five hundred beer-related events, including food pairing dinners at top restaurants, beer-making classes, meet-the-brewer sessions, and educational experiences. Tasty gluten-free beer, anyone? Chocolate and beer pairings? It's all here, and more.

sdbw.sdbeer.com

ELEVATE YOUR BRUNCH GAME
AT MORNING GLORY

For outrageous, Instagram-worthy decor and breakfast ideas that span the globe, ascend the stairs to this $4 million brunch-only spot named for a plant with hallucinogenic properties. That is, once you get through the line to get in: no reservations are accepted at Morning Glory, and don't even bother calling with questions. Inside, a giant pink neon starburst hovers overhead, pink and black tile stretches underfoot, and handsome windows facing the morning sun adjust to let in the breeze. The vending machine is stocked with Moët & Chandon and a tableside cart has makings for Bloody Marys topped with celery foam. The menu hopscotches from Japanese soufflé pancakes to Georgian khachapuri and slides from pork belly fried rice to fried chicken and waffles. Brunch at Morning Glory is one cheerful millennial acid trip.

550 W. Date St., 619-629-0302
morningglorybreakfast.com
Neighborhood: Little Italy

RELISH THE ROYALE
—WITH CHEESE

As in most American cities, the lowly hamburger has staged an epic revival in San Diego over the last decade. Whether offered on the sly at a gourmet establishment or at the beloved California chain In-N-Out, the options for a tasty burger are endless. For me, Royale hits the spot with its charming, unpretentious retro ambience coupled with a bar primed by adult beverages for garnish. Go all in on a Royale with Cheese, embellished with bacon, caramelized onions, gruyere, mustard, and pickles on a toasted buttermilk bun. The Diner Burger is a straightforward quarter-pounder topped with American cheese, lettuce, and special sauce on a sesame seed bun—for pure simplicity, this is what a Big Mac aspires to. Royale uses only grass-fed organic beef, the sesame seed buns are baked fresh daily, and produce is supplied by the owner's farm.

4204 Voltaire St., 619-431-5653
royalesd.com
Neighborhood: Between Point Loma and Ocean Beach

FIVE OTHER BURGER JOINTS (AND RESTAURANTS) WORTH TRYING

Jayne's Gastropub

4677 Thirtieth St., 619-563-1011, jaynesgastropub.com
Neighborhood: North Park

Crazee Burger

3993 Thirtieth St., 619-282-6044, crazeeburger.com
Neighborhood: North Park

Bankers Hill Bar & Restaurant

2202 Fourth Ave., 619-231-0222, bankershillsd.com
Neighborhood: Bankers Hill

Starlite

3175 India St., 619-358-9766, starlitesandiego.com
Neighborhood: Midtown

Public House La Jolla

830 Kline St., 858-551-9210, the-publichouse.com
Neighborhood: La Jolla

DEVOUR AN ASIAN FEAST
ON CONVOY STREET

A series of crowded, unassuming strip malls tucked between car dealerships along Convoy Street in Kearny Mesa accommodates a dizzying concentration of Asian cuisines. You could easily spend a week tasting all the different cultures and cuisines for lunch and dinner, ranging from Vietnamese to Japanese to Thai to Chinese, with a stop in Hong Kong for good measure. Among the several dozen eateries, try Tofu House for its Korean warm tofu soup, Phuong Trang Vietnamese for salt and pepper shrimp and whole fried catfish, and Facing East Noodle Bar for Taiwanese dishes such as braised duck noodle soup or pork and chive dumplings, but leave room for the freakshake—a milkshake crowned with donuts, peanut butter pretzels, sea urchin cotton candy and other whimsical add-ons.

Between Clairemont Mesa Blvd. and Aero Dr.
Neighborhood: Kearny Mesa

QUENCH YOUR POLYNESIAN FANTASIES
WITH A BALI HAI MAI TAI

Family owned and operated since 1954, Bali Hai is renowned for San Diego's most iconic cocktail, the Mai Tai—more than 2.6 million have been sold to date. The popular restaurant boasts that their recipe for the tropical concoction is fruit-free. Instead, bartenders mix Coruba Jamaican Dark Rum, Ron Castillo Light Rum, a dash of orange liqueur, a dash of Trader Vic's orgeat syrup, and a splash of sweet and sour, delivering an oversized and powerfully potent libation. To heighten the experience, this expansive tiki temple offers a sweeping panorama of San Diego Bay and the downtown skyline amid hand-carved sculptures, tapa cloths, and other Polynesian artifacts. The menu offers up South Pacific delicacies like coconut shrimp, Hawaiian tuna poke, and lobster wonton tacos, along with a fleet of surf and turf favorites.

2230 Shelter Island Dr., 619-222-1181
balihairestaurant.com
Neighborhood: Shelter Island

George's Ocean Terrace

REEL IN FISH TACOS FOR LUNCH
AT RUBIO'S

Without a doubt, San Diego's one indispensable fast food is the humble fish taco. Credit a local surfer, Ralph Rubio, for the "research" he put into tasting fish tacos out of thatched-roof beach shacks in Baja. The recipe he brought home and popularized was batter-dipped, deep-fried fish (now Alaskan pollock) folded in corn tortillas and garnished with shredded cabbage, salsa, and tangy *crema* sauce. Starting in 1983, the tacos caught on, and today you'll find Rubio's Coastal Grill in two hundred locations throughout California and the West. Menus at the fast-casual restaurants have expanded to include other Mexican dishes, and beer and wine are served, but with 249 million sold to date, need I tell you what the most popular item is?

4504 E. Mission Bay Dr., 858-272-2801, rubios.com
Neighborhood: Pacific Beach, (but locations throughout San Diego)

TIP
So ubiquitous is the fish taco to San Diego that it's a staple on many restaurant menus. For a gourmet take with a dreamy rooftop view, head to George's Ocean Terrace, where the tacos are made with grilled cod and topped with green papaya slaw, mango-habañero salsa, cilantro and crema. 1250 Prospect Street, La Jolla, 858-454-4244, georgesatthecove.com.

San Diego Symphony conductor Rafael Payare.
Photo courtesy of San Diego Symphony.

MUSIC AND ENTERTAINMENT

GROOVE TO LIVE JAMS
AT BELLY UP TAVERN

Occupying a funky Quonset Hut in Solana Beach, the Belly Up Tavern has hosted critically acclaimed artists of all genres for more than forty-five years. On any given night, the music ranges from Etta James to 10,000 Maniacs, Death Cab for Cutie to Rufus Wainwright—plus up-and-coming artists playing alternative rock, reggae, jazz, Latin, and more. Even the Rolling Stones took the stage once here in 2015 for an unadvertised concert. The six-hundred-seat venue is intimate yet comfortable, catering to regulars with inoffensive drink prices. For those who want to dodge the thirty-minute drive from downtown, the Coaster commuter rail stop is just two blocks away, and the adjacent Wild Note Café serves a fusion of Pacific Coast flavors before and after the show. Advance tickets, recommended, are available through the website and at the box office.

143 S. Cedros Ave., 858-481-8140
bellyup.com
Neighborhood: Solana Beach

BEND YOUR EAR
FOR SUMMER POPS
AT SAN DIEGO SYMPHONY'S SHELL

Long a fixture of the summer outdoor music scene, the San Diego Symphony built a permanent outdoor concert venue in 2020. Known as the Shell, this stage is the only such waterfront facility on the West Coast. Trimmed by the lights of downtown, the Shell provides sophisticated acoustics in a park-like setting next to San Diego Bay. Summer "pops" concerts by the acclaimed San Diego Symphony cover a range of genres—from classical to Broadway, and jazz to R&B. On some nights, movies from series like *Harry Potter* and *Star Wars* are presented with live orchestral accompaniment; on others, tributes to musical treasures like The Beatles or Miles Davis are featured. Designer picnics by prominent local chefs are available from stands at the rear of the venue (tip: bring a sweater for cool bayside nights). Copley Symphony Hall, also downtown, hosts the orchestra's regular season October through May.

206 Marina Park Way, 619-235-0804
sandiegosymphony.org
Neighborhood: Downtown

PURR WITH THE FELINES
OF SAN DIEGO ZOO

More than 3,500 creatures representing 650 animal species reside at this celebrated and influential zoo in a lush, expansive nook within Balboa Park. Animal lovers will find more than enough to fill an entire day, especially once they land at the spectacular addition, Africa Rocks. The $68 million project transformed one canyon into habitats that spotlight Africa's biodiversity, ranging from penguins to leopards and from meerkats to baboons. Smart visitors to this world's most-visited animal sanctuary embark on one of several specialty tours offered on select days, such as Crazy About Cats, a two-hour exploration behind the scenes to visit some of the most iconic cat species. Private visits with a rotating list of marquee stars include a jaguar, lion, tiger, mountain lion, fishing cat, ocelot, and a serval.

2920 Zoo Dr., 619-231-1515
sandiegozoo.com
Neighborhood: Balboa Park

FIVE MORE REASONS THE SAN DIEGO ZOO IS NOT JUST ANY ZOO

San Diego Zoo founder Dr. Harry Wegeforth brought home plants from every location where the animals were acquired, to create a more authentic natural environment. With more than 700,000 plants, the flora from such a large variety of climate zones are said to be worth more than the animal collection.

The hundred-acre zoo was at the forefront of the move toward "cageless" environments, using moats to separate animals from humans rather than wire or fence. Some of the largest free-flight aviaries anywhere are here, allowing guests to enter giant cages to observe colorful birds in close proximity in a naturalistic setting.

Many species housed here are extremely rare. Only sixty Amur leopards are thought to exist in the wild in Russia and Northern China, but a pair lives here. The strange platypus, an egg-laying mammal, is found nowhere outside Australia except the zoo's Safari Park.

The zoo is involved with animal preservation in forty-five countries around the world and has engineered many "firsts" in breeding—from the nearly-extinct California condor to recently discovered Visayan warty pigs—and 180 rhinos have been born at the zoo's Safari Park.

Beyond fast-food options, Albert's Restaurant is like a treehouse oasis. Offering sit-down dining of a quality beyond the snack-bar fare you get at most zoos, it's a great place to break up your visit for a midday snack (when your kids and the animals are laziest).

ROAR AND SNORE WITH THE BEASTIES
AT SAN DIEGO ZOO SAFARI PARK

The African safari is a bucket-list journey for most of us, but at the San Diego Zoo Safari Park you can sleep in a tent in close proximity to giraffes, rhinos, and antelope. After checking in for Roar and Snore, you can take an after-hours guided walk to observe the animals' nocturnal life. After-dinner campfire tales are punctuated by eerie animal calls emanating from the dark corners of the park. Enjoy a pancake breakfast in the morning and take the day to see the rest of the park. The 1,800-acre safari park thirty-three miles north of downtown is well worth visiting even if you don't spend the night. More than three thousand animals, interacting much as they would in the wild, live in the sprawling enclosures designed to replicate environments like African forests and Australian grasslands.

15500 San Pasqual Valley Rd., Escondido, 760-747-8702
sdzsafaripark.org
Neighborhood: San Pasqual Valley

TIP

The cloudiest months of the year in San Diego come at the end of spring, lasting into early summer. If you explore San Diego during this time period, you can look forward to hearing the local excuses of "May Gray" and "June Gloom." Solution: head away from the coast where the marine layer lingers longest. The Safari Park, located about sixteen miles inland, is usually sunny and warm for most of the day, even during our grayest months.

ENJOY TOP TOURING ACTS
AT HUMPHREY'S CONCERTS BY THE BAY

Beloved by San Diegans and visiting performers alike, Humphrey's is a 1,400-seat outdoor venue sandwiched between bobbing yachts in a Shelter Island marina and a Polynesian-themed hotel. The unique ambience induces performers to return again and again—Ray Charles is said to have performed at Humphrey's thirty-seven times. The acts run the gamut, from Tony Bennett to Bill Maher and from John Legend to Bob Dylan, attracting multiple generations of attendees since its opening in 1982. The annual season runs from May through September, though a few acts sneak in just before and after. Tickets are sold at the box office and through Ticketmaster, but note that the best seats—the first eight or so rows—are usually reserved for those buying a dinner-and-show package with the adjacent restaurant (also called Humphrey's).

2241 Shelter Island Dr., 619-224-3577
humphreysconcerts.com
Neighborhood: Point Loma

TIP
Humphrey's features prominently in the moving, Oscar-winning 2013 documentary, *20 Feet from Stardom.*

DON YOUR BEST DRAG FOR AN EVENING
AT LIPS

Now that RuPaul has made drag less racy and more acceptable to the masses, gather up your sartorial glam for an evening out with the queens at Lips, the nation's largest drag cabaret chain. Here, performance and art combine with wit to conquer prejudices in a brightly colored setting full of glittering disco balls and shimmering chandeliers. Every night is a different show, like Thursday's Dinner with the divas or the Dragalicious Gospel Brunch on Sundays hosted by Sister Nun-of-the-Above. On a typical night, you'll be sharing Lips with bachelorette parties, birthday celebrations, and maybe an engagement or divorce—the crew will help you toast any occasion. But be forewarned: part of the entertainment is watching blushing brides-to-be and others getting hauled onstage to be alternately harassed and heralded by the drag queens. Reservations required.

3036 El Cajon Blvd., 619-295-7900
lipssd.com
Neighborhood: North Park

REJOICE IN CHRISTMAS
AT THE SAN DIEGO PARADE OF LIGHTS

In early December, for two consecutive Sundays, San Diego Bay is lit up like a Christmas tree during the San Diego Parade of Lights. Cheered on by 100,000 spectators, dozens of boats of all shapes and sizes follow a parade route beginning at Shelter Island and passing Harbor Island, the Embarcadero, Seaport Village, and Ferry Landing in Coronado. Since 1971, this tradition has become synonymous with the holiday season in San Diego, with all manner of private vessels participating, decorated to the gills. Judges score each boat based on lighting, music, special effects, and originality, with prizes that are worth the effort. While it's fun to experience the show on the water, there are lots of great locations for landlubbers along the route, including many restaurants along Harbor Island, the Embarcadero, and in Coronado.

1220 Rosecrans St., Suite 414, 619-224-2240
sdparadeoflights.org
Neighborhoods: Downtown, Point Loma, Coronado

FLIRT WITH SEADRAGONS AND SEAHORSES
AT BIRCH AQUARIUM

Killer whales? Been there. Elephants? Done that. Sometimes it's the most demure critters that pack the biggest wallop, and the recently expanded Seadragons & Seahorses exhibit at the Birch Aquarium will have you swooning with delight. The seadragons and seahorses cavort in the aquarium's giant new tank, while a behind-the-scenes tour immerses guests in the facility's ongoing, twenty-five-year seahorse research program. Birch, the public side of the world-renowned Scripps Institution of Oceanography, is the leader in seahorse and (as of 2020) seadragon breeding conservation, but there's much more to see. With around sixty habitats representing various Pacific Ocean environments such as tide pools and a giant kelp forest, creatures on display range from fierce tiger sharks to garibaldi (California's state marine fish), and from fanciful white anemones to voluptuous moon jellies. There are also absorbing interpretive exhibits on cutting-edge research at Scripps.

2300 Expedition Way, 858-534-3474
aquarium.ucsd.edu
Neighborhood: La Jolla Shores

TAKE ME OUT TO A PADRES GAME
AT PETCO PARK

The San Diego Padres' home field is one of the most thoughtfully designed, aesthetically pleasing Major League ballparks—a retro classic planted right in the center of bustling downtown. How many other teams have a left field foul pole at the corner of a 111-year-old building? The brick walls of the four-story Western Metal Supply Co. warehouse serve as a prominent fixture, along with six other historic buildings. None of this impedes great sightlines, coupled with views of the city skyline, the bay, and Balboa Park. And while the 42,300-seat Petco Park isn't the first to offer sushi alongside franks and fries, you'll also find authentic Neapolitan pizza out of a brick oven, a barbecue stand run by former Padres pitcher Randy Jones, and mouth-watering carnitas tacos—plus the best lineup of craft beers in the majors. Check out the Park in the Park, a grassy slope behind the outfield offering bargain admission (ideal for young children).

100 Park Blvd., 619-795-5000, mlb.com/padres
Neighborhood: Downtown

TIP
Petco Park-ing is costly. Consider taking the trolley, which makes three stops a short walk from the park entrances.

ROCK
AT THE CASBAH

San Diego's most iconic location for indie rock, this intimate venue on the edge of Little Italy has been discovering local and national talent since 1989, hosting such legends as Nirvana, The Arcade Fire, The White Stripes, and Smashing Pumpkins before they hit it big. Don't look for such names today—the Casbah has a capacity of just two hundred—but because the management books much bigger stages around town such as The Observatory, do come here for authentic discoveries in an unfiltered dive bar environment. There are cheap drinks, a back room with pool tables and pinball, and an outdoor patio where you can enjoy the stars between acts. Lines are long nearly every night for up-and-coming touring acts as well as more popular local groups—get on the mailing list to access tickets as soon as they're released.

2501 Kettner Blvd., 619-232-4355
casbahmusic.com
Neighborhood: Little Italy

MEET A SEA CANARY
AT SEAWORLD

The SeaWorld theme park empire got its start in San Diego in 1964, but as the parks have multiplied over the years, the marine focus has taken a back seat to roller coasters. However, peel back the thrill-ride veneer and you'll find solid animal encounters, including a few that go beyond pirouetting dolphins and fluke flinging killer whales. Interaction with the affable beluga whales inside their watery habitat is one example. Guests wearing wetsuits are allowed to touch and feed these sociable white whales. Nicknamed "sea canaries" for their cheerful calls, belugas are listed as threatened or endangered in the Arctic, their natural environment. Afterward, check out the park's five hundred other species, including the only emperor penguin colony in the western hemisphere and Shark Reef, home to sand tiger, bonnethead, blacktip, and whitetip reef sharks.

500 SeaWorld Dr., 619-222-4732
seaworldsandiego.com
Neighborhood: Mission Bay

SEEK YOUR FORTUNE IN SAN DIEGO'S BACKCOUNTRY
AT A CASINO RESORT

With the largest concentration of Native American tribes of any county in the United States—eighteen in all—San Diego's backcountry has an array of bustling casino resorts. The first of the casinos was built by the Sycuan people, a simple bingo palace that opened in 1983. In 2019, the Sycuan Band completed a $260 million project to create a Vegas-style casino hotel and resort. In addition to 302 hotel rooms in a 12-story tower, the expansion includes a spa and fitness center, cabana-lined pool and lazy river, and an enlarged gaming floor with 2,800 slot machines and 80 table games. Non-smokers can enjoy slots and table games and other amenities in a new smoke-free environment. In addition to a steakhouse, San Diego favorites like Hodad's, Phil's BBQ, Lucha Libre, and Luna Grill are available in the UnCommons, a marketplace for casual dining.

5469 Casino Way, El Cajon, 800-279-2826
sycuan.com
Neighborhood: Harbison Canyon

KID AROUND
AT LEGOLAND

The world's most famous plastic building blocks get their due at Legoland California, nirvana for most eight-year-olds (and for a few adults who still cherish their Lego days). Beautifully landscaped with bonsai trees, the 128-acre park is chock-full of gentle rides and pint-sized roller coasters, with world landmarks recreated from Legos, a miniature golf course, and a Star Wars Miniland. A new attraction that debuted in 2020 is Lego Movie World, inspired by the Lego film franchise and featuring a "flying" theatre. In all, 60 million Lego bricks were employed to create this whimsical fantasyland. There's a water park for splashy fun, and the Sea Life Aquarium—with real, not plastic, fish—is right next door (separate admissions required). While teens may find Legoland a bit of a snooze, it's a must-see for kids ages 2 to 12.

1 Legoland Dr., 760-918-5346
legoland.com/california
Neighborhood: Carlsbad

TIP

When Legoland opens, many visitors hop
in line for the first two rides encountered
(neither of which is very special). Therefore,
it's better to head to the back side of the park
where lines are shorter for the first hour or so.

DANCE THE NIGHT AWAY
AT OMNIA

Close proximity to both Hollywood and Las Vegas helps make downtown San Diego's nightlife one of the buzzier scenes on the West Coast, and much of it is centered in the historic Gaslamp Quarter. Trendiest of all the venues is Omnia, a spinoff of the same club in Vegas offering three distinct experiences and vantage points for clubgoers to enjoy the sights and sounds: an eight-thousand-square-foot main dance area, a large balcony gazing onto the scene, and an outdoor terrace overlooking the Gaslamp Quarter with an additional dance floor, tiered cabanas, and sofas under the stars. With a state-of-the-art sound system and mind-bending lighting, Omnia hosts celebrity DJs and live performances, and otherwise spins a variety of musical genres from electronic and Top 40 artists.

454 Sixth Ave., 619-544-9500
omniaclubs.com/san-diego
Neighborhood: Downtown

REVEL IN THE ADULT ANTICS OF OVER-THE-LINE

Sure, San Diego may not have a professional football team to cheer on but the city can still point to Over-the-Line as a sporting event its residents excel at. An informal novelty game started by members of the Old Mission Beach Athletic Club in the 1950s, the annual tournament gathers 1,200 or more teams for two weekends of bawdy revelry in mid-July. Similar to baseball, three-person Over-the-Line teams include a batter, pitcher, and fielder, and the court is any available patch of sand. The annual tournament divides teams by gender and age (some players are well into their eighties). Beer is involved, there's a lot of skin in this game, and team names sometimes swing toward the wildly inappropriate, which is why minors are discouraged from attending.

Fiesta Island
ombac.org/over-the-line/
Neighborhood: Mission Bay

SAIL AWAY TO DISTANT HORIZONS
FROM THE PORT OF SAN DIEGO

It takes a lot to lure locals away from San Diego, but cruise lines tempt us with over a hundred sailings annually seeking far-flung ports. The city's dominant lines are Carnival Cruises (*Carnival Miracle* is home-ported in San Diego for most of the year), Disney Cruises (*Disney Wonder* is home-ported here) and Holland America Line. While most of the itineraries are four- and five-night roundtrip cruises beginning in fall and continuing through spring to the Mexican Riviera (Cabo San Lucas, Mazatlán, Puerto Vallarta), there are longer and more exotic journeys available. Two-week voyages to Hawaii and one-way Caribbean itineraries via the Panama Canal are common, and in April a number of cruise lines reposition ships for the Alaskan season, resulting in bargains on one-way cruises from San Diego to Seattle or Vancouver. Then in October, the trip is offered in reverse.

1140 N. Harbor Dr., 619-400-4744
portofsandiego.org/experiences/plan-your-cruise
Neighborhood: Downtown

WANDER THROUGH THE FLOWER FIELDS
OF CARLSBAD

Carlsbad and neighboring Encinitas represent a noteworthy commercial flower-growing region, and each spring a beguiling panoply of color can be seen at the Flower Fields, a hillside event venue that has been home to a spectacular flower display since the 1950s. Growers from Carlsbad Ranch spend months preparing the fields with a meticulously planned palette, filling fifty acres with thousands of Giant Tecolote Ranunculus flowers. A member of the buttercup family, the flower remains in bloom for up to ten weeks, from early March to mid-May. A quarter-million visitors flock to the fields each year to walk amid the vibrant landscape, and there are also rose and theme gardens, fresh strawberries, a cymbidium greenhouse, a poinsettia display, a sweet pea maze, and antique tractor wagon rides. Picnicking is allowed, and if you have any energy left afterward, there is shopping at the nearby Carlsbad Premium Outlets.

5704 Paseo Del Norte, 760-431-0352
theflowerfields.com
Neighborhood: Carlsbad

MARCH FOR INDEPENDENCE DAY AND THE BIG BAY BOOM

Coronado, home to a sizeable contingent of military veterans, throws one of the most popular Independence Day celebrations in the nation. The first parade was held in 1888, and it's been an annual tradition since the 1940s. Today, upwards of a half-million people attend, and residents and visitors alike start lining the Orange Avenue parade route before dawn. The first activity is a 12K run at 7:00 a.m., followed by a Rough Water Swim event. The parade starts at 10:00 a.m. with a patriotic naval presence in the floats and bands, then for the rest of the day, an art show and concert attract the crowds to Spreckels Park. While there are fireworks at Coronado's Glorietta Bay, the big show is hosted by San Diego, where one of the nation's largest fireworks displays—dubbed the Big Bay Boom—blooms.

1100 Orange Ave., 866-599-7242
coronado.ca.us
Neighborhoods: Coronado and San Diego Bay

TIP

The Big Bay Boom is launched simultaneously from four barges around North San Diego Bay. The show can be seen from Shelter Island, Harbor Island, the Embarcadero, Marina District, Seaport Village, and Coronado Ferry Landing.

Paragliding at Torrey
Pines Gliderport

SPORTS AND RECREATION

HONOR THE UNDEVELOPED CALIFORNIA COASTLINE
AT TORREY PINES

The three-hundred-foot-high seafront cliffs rising from beaches north of La Jolla are home to Torrey Pines State Natural Reserve, a 1,500-acre park that shelters North America's rarest pine trees. Found only here and on a small island 175 miles northwest of the city, the trees are inelegant and gnarled characters clinging precariously to water-carved sandstone bluffs. The reserve is also one of the last precious parcels of undeveloped southern California coastline, encompassing the beach below and a lagoon immediately north. Wildlife includes red-tailed hawks, California quail, black-tailed jackrabbits, and coyotes. On fog-shrouded spring mornings visitors are rewarded with a dazzle of wildflowers. Stop by the visitor center, an old adobe lodge inspired by Hopi dwellings, to get info on a half-dozen trails up to 1.4 miles in length.

12600 N. Torrey Pines Rd., 858-755-2063
torreypine.org
Neighborhood: Torrey Pines

TIP
A few restrictions are in place to help preserve the reserve. No food is allowed at Torrey Pines, except on the beach near the entrance, where there are trashcans. Smoking, dogs, and drones are also not allowed.

CYCLE THE BAYSHORE BIKEWAY

Many of San Diego's cycling routes involve hills, but the twenty-four-mile Bayshore Bikeway offers a flat, breezy trip around San Diego Bay, and most of it is on dedicated paths, away from traffic. You can ride the horseshoe-shaped circuit in either direction, but I recommend picking up a hybrid, road, or electric bike downtown at Wheel Fun Rentals and taking the ferry south to Coronado, then looping counter-clockwise around the bay. Wend your way through resort-y Coronado past the iconic Hotel del Coronado to the Silver Strand, an isthmus of dunes linking the island to Imperial Beach, California's southernmost beach community. At the southern end of the bay, the hills of Tijuana float on the horizon, while the water sparkles like diamonds courtesy of the salt crystals harvested here. Circling north, you'll pass a national wildlife refuge, the naval shipyard, and colorful murals at Chicano Park.

1355 N. Harbor Dr., 619-324-7244
wheelfunrentals.com
Neighborhoods: Downtown/Coronado/Chula Vista

TIP

Avid cyclists can complete the circuit in a couple of hours, but casual riders will want to allow most of the day for the journey back to downtown. Alternately, a counter-clockwise route will allow you to hop onto the San Diego Trolley at the Palomar Street Transit Center, shaving off the last ten miles.

RENDEZVOUS WITH CETACEANS
ON A WHALE-WATCHING TOUR

Starting in early December, twenty thousand gray whales migrate each year from the summer feeding grounds of Alaska to the calm calving lagoons of Baja California, passing close to San Diego. From February through April, they head north again on their six-thousand-mile journey, with calves in tow. Accompanied by a trained naturalist, meet up with these forty- to fifty-foot behemoths aboard one of Hornblower Cruises' whale and dolphin watching adventures and enjoy watching these gentle creatures swimming gracefully and resolutely through the ocean. The cruises start near the Broadway Pier and journey out through the bay into the open ocean beyond Point Loma. Bonus: in recent years blue whales—typically found in deeper waters—have begun feeding on krill along the California coast in summer. Check out earth's largest creature, along with occasional killer whales, on these summer tours.

970 N. Harbor Dr., 619-430-2338
hornblower.com
Neighborhood: Downtown

TIP

For a more intimate whale-watching experience, climb aboard Next Level Sailing's *The America*, a replica of a 139-foot yacht built in 1850 that some call the world's most famous racing yacht. Gray whales are the focus in winter, while humpbacks arrive in March. In summer, lucky visitors may encounter the largest animal on the planet, the blue whale, weighing up to 300,000 pounds. nextlevelsailing.com

DIVE WRECK ALLEY

Although the Southern California coastline is famed for its towering kelp forests, another thrill for divers is Wreck Alley, so named for the ship carcasses collecting right off the shores of Mission Beach. The headliner is the HMCS *Yukon*, a 366-foot Canadian destroyer escort that was sunk in 2000. Intact and sitting at a depth of between seventy and a hundred feet, the wreck is home to plenty of marine life, with swim-throughs and penetration opportunities. Nearby is the *Ruby E.*, a weathered, 166-foot Coast Guard cutter lying upright about eighty feet below, and the NOSC (Naval Oceans Systems Center) Tower, an anemone-encrusted research installation that looks much like a small oil rig and reaches within thirty feet of the surface. Waterhorse Charters takes scuba-certified divers here and to other top sites, such as the Point Loma kelp forests and the Islas los Coronados off Tijuana.

1617 Quivira Road, Ste. B, 619-224-6195
waterhorsecharters.com
Neighborhood: Mission Bay

LOOK BEFORE YOU LEAP INTO THE VOID
AT TORREY PINES GLIDERPORT

San Diego's aviation history is robust: from the *Spirit of St. Louis*, built here in 1927, to the US Navy's Topgun training established at Naval Station Miramar, the region is full of firsts. As such, seafront Torrey Pines Gliderport—where Charles Lindbergh once trained— is a great place for novices to take a first, thrilling paraglide flight, especially when winds are at their gusty best from March through June. You'll strap yourself into a bucket seat in front of an experienced pilot, inch toward the edge of bluffs that drop 372 feet to the tawny sands of Black's Beach, and as wind fills the elliptical wing, you'll soar heavenward. The tandem flight ($175) involves figure-eight loops along the edge of the cliff for about thirty minutes, resulting in a ride that's more deeply rewarding than any theme park roller coaster.

2800 Torrey Pines Scenic Dr., 858-452-9858
flytorrey.com
Neighborhood: Torrey Pines

TIP
If the idea of stepping off the edge of a cliff puts you in a sweat, ogle the scene from the Cliffhanger Café and watch as other crazy aviators jump off the cliff.

PAMPER YOUR POOCH
AT DOG BEACH

When dogs dream of heaven, the scene probably looks a bit like Dog Beach, a stretch of sand at the north end of Ocean Beach designated in 1972 as one of the nation's first official leash-free beaches. Once paws hit the sand, the leashes come off and the running, splashing, fetching, posing, and socializing begins. Water fountains, doggie bags, and even tennis balls and toys are available. In short, Dog Beach is a joy for canines—a melting pot for dogs of all sizes, shapes, colors, creeds, and breeds. Most of the nearby bars and restaurants are dog-friendly, but after playing in the sand and saltwater surf, you'll probably want a bath for Rover, so head to nearby Dog Beach Dog Wash (4933 Voltaire Street, 619-523-1700) where you'll find specialty shampoos along with grooming and nail trimming services.

5156W W. Point Loma Blvd., 619-221-8899
dogbeachsd.com
Neighborhood: Ocean Beach

STRIP TO YOUR BIRTHDAY SUIT
AT BLACK'S BEACH

On San Diego's curious roster of firsts is the nation's earliest public clothing-optional beach. While the era of legal nude sunbathing on the city-managed portion of Black's Beach lasted only a few years during the mid-1970s, the character of this secluded and beautiful shoreline was firmly established. What has kept Black's special is the difficulty of reaching this two-mile-long stretch of sand. You either have to clamber down one of two ill-maintained trails descending the three-hundred-foot bluffs at the Torrey Pines Gliderport—one steep, the other steeper—or you need to meander more than a mile along the shoreline from the closest road access points at either end (one at La Jolla Shores, the other at the Torrey Pines State Beach parking lot). Note that there are no facilities and few lifeguards, but citations for nudity are rare.

12000 block of N. Torrey Pines Rd.
Neighborhood: Torrey Pines

SKATE BY THE SEA
AT THE HOTEL DEL CORONADO

Who says it's 72 degrees year-round in San Diego? Each December, the historic Hotel del Coronado transforms into a lavish holiday wonderland featuring beautiful decorations, including a giant Christmas tree in the main lobby and thousands of white lights adorning the historic Victorian building and grounds. With activities scheduled for guests of all ages, the most uniquely Southern California experience is The Del's Skating by the Sea, featuring beachfront ice skating with the Pacific Ocean tossing nearby. The scene is created by converting the oceanfront Windsor Lawn—wedding central for most of the year— into a spectacular ice rink, starting the week prior to Thanksgiving and running through New Year's Day. The skating is a splurge, but watching is free, and the event comes complete with fire pits, holiday music, and drinks to warm you up.

1500 Orange Ave., 619-435-6611
hoteldel.com
Neighborhood: Coronado

HIKE MT. WOODSON
(AND TAKE A BITE OF POTATO CHIP ROCK)

High atop Mount Woodson is a visually delicious natural rock formation that has become an Instagram icon. Aptly named Potato Chip Rock, the wafer-thin granite formation protrudes from just below the summit and into the otherwise sweeping view of Poway and the Blue Sky Ecological Preserve. Along the trail that leads to it are lots of cracks and bouldering problems for climbers to tackle. The exposed hike from the Lake Poway trailhead involves a 7.6-mile round trip and an elevation gain exceeding two thousand feet, so the ascent is not for sissies. In summer, the ranger station reports regular heat stroke rescues of hikers who aren't carrying the recommended two liters of water per person. But the journey is worth the time, and you'll come home having taken advantage of a photo op with a social media icon to share with your friends.

Trailhead: 14644 Lake Poway Rd., 858-668-4772
poway.org
Neighborhood: Poway

TIP
A shorter hike to the summit takes the Mt. Woodson Road—closed to private vehicles—up the east flank of the mountain from Highway 67.

Stars & Stripes

SAIL THE AMERICA'S CUP RACING YACHT, *STARS & STRIPES*

San Diego is one of the very few places where you can sail an authentic America's Cup yacht—in this case *Stars & Stripes* (USA-11), the eleventh boat built and sailed (in 1992) by San Diego yachtsman Dennis Conner, three-time winner of the Cup. You'll cruise the calm, wind-ruffled waters of San Diego Bay, making lots of exciting tacks and jibes. Everyone gets to grind the winches to raise and trim the sails, handle the lines, and even take a turn at the helm. The three-hour, interactive excursion runs almost daily in summer and at least twice a week in winter (always on Saturdays). As each sailing is limited to twenty-four passengers, reservations are essential. A photographer is on board for the cruise, and links to photos and videos are included in the price.

1551 Shelter Island Dr., 619-255-4705
sailusa11.com
Neighborhood: Point Loma

RUN WITH THE GRUNIONS

No, this is not some new marathon, nor a creature from Seuss-land. Grunions are a slippery little fish unique to Southern California and Northern Baja, and for a few months each year their odd nighttime mating ritual provides a delightful show to those in the know. On select nights, the slender, silvery fish ride waves onto the wet beach, where they writhe and wriggle, burrowing and spawning before returning to the sea. The runs only happen a couple of hours after high tide during the two days before and after a full or new moon, from March through September. At its peak, the sand can be covered with thousands of the little critters and collecting grunions to fry up a late-night snack is a favorite San Diego pastime (no collection is allowed in April or May though, and note that a fishing license is required to scoop up the fish).

wildlife.ca.gov/Fishing/Ocean/Grunion
Neighborhoods: Ocean Beach, Mission Beach, La Jolla Shores,
Coronado Beach and Silver Strand

MUSS YOUR HAIR AND RATTLE YOUR BONES
ON THE GIANT DIPPER

Built in 1925 during the golden age of wooden roller coasters, the Giant Dipper at Belmont Park is a vintage seafront coaster that still packs a thrill (hopefully not ending with a visit to the chiropractor!). First opened on July 4, 1925, the park's zenith was in the early 1930s, when riders paid just 15 cents to roll along the dips and turns. Although the park fell on hard times over the ensuing decades, the coaster was restored at a cost of $2 million in 1990 and declared a national historic landmark. Special day passes are available which provide access to many of Belmont Park's other attractions, including carnival-style rides, a climbing wall, zip line, arcades, go-carts, bumper cars, miniature golf, and a three-level *Tron*-themed laser-tag arena. Belmont Park is ideal for families, friends, and parties for every occasion.

3146 Mission Blvd., 858-228-9283
belmontpark.com
Neighborhood: Mission Beach

TRACK DOWN A DEEP-FRIED TWINKIE
AT THE SAN DIEGO COUNTY FAIR

Drawing more than 1.5 million attendees annually, San Diego boasts the largest county fair in the US. The month-long event, held at the Del Mar Fairgrounds and traditionally ending on the Fourth of July, began in 1880 as a way to bring local farmers together to share ideas, compete for prizes for the best pies and produce, and challenge one another on horseback. While the fair continues to celebrate agriculture and community pride, it has grown into a multifaceted entertainment mecca featuring animal and farm exhibits, local and national musical performers, retail and hobby tents, carnival rides, and the most calorie-packed food choices imaginable. You'll want to set aside an entire day and evening for your visit to cover all the fair has to offer. Just be prepared for traffic snarls going and coming, especially on weekends.

2260 Jimmy Durante Blvd., 858-755-1161
sdfair.com
Neighborhood: Del Mar

LEARN HOW TO RIDE THE WAVES
WITH A SURF DIVA

You probably know that San Diego is home to some of the best waves on the West Coast. If you're already comfortable on a surfboard, you'll find popular breaks at Tourmaline Surf Park in Pacific Beach, at Windansea, and along the Silver Strand. Many area surf shops rent gear, and the best waves land from August through November. La Jolla Shores has gentler waves, and this is where world-famous surf school Surf Diva offers private and group lessons for surfers of all ages and ability levels, taught by professional instructors. It's the largest school on the West Coast, and the instructors place a special emphasis on teaching women and girls (although men are, of course, welcome, too!). Teenagers especially will delight in the school's boutique, stocked with the latest beach fashions including Surf Diva's own line of swim and active wear.

2160 Avenida de la Playa, 858-454-8273
surfdiva.com
Neighborhood: La Jolla Shores

AMBLE ALONG SUNSET CLIFFS
FOR DREAMY SEASIDE VISTAS

San Diego's loveliest sunset stroll passes along the edge of aptly named Sunset Cliffs, the rugged coastline that bridges the Ocean Beach and Point Loma neighborhoods. Perfect for families with kids, snuggling lovers, or solo types looking for a backdrop for introspection, the path follows Sunset Cliffs Boulevard as it winds south along the wave-sculpted cliffs for 1.5 miles. Start from the Inn at Sunset Cliffs—parking along the road is usually available just beyond the Inn. Surfers often ply the gnarly waves, and the inland side is fronted by one beautiful—often historic—house after another. There's a sixty-eight-acre park at Ladera Street where you'll find natural arches and sea caves. Don't wander close to the cliff edge; the slowly eroding bluffs have claimed many lives over the decades.

Sunset Cliffs Boulevard
sandiego.gov/park-and-recreation/parks/regional/shoreline/sunset

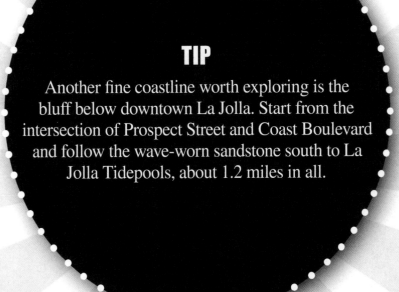

TIP

Another fine coastline worth exploring is the bluff below downtown La Jolla. Start from the intersection of Prospect Street and Coast Boulevard and follow the wave-worn sandstone south to La Jolla Tidepools, about 1.2 miles in all.

Kayaking in La Jolla

PADDLE WITH WHALES AND SEA LIONS AND SHARKS, OH MY!

San Diego's number one adventure tour suitable for all ages is kayaking through the La Jolla Ecological Reserve to La Jolla's sea caves. No previous kayak experience is necessary to enjoy sea lions sunbathing on the rocks up close, and witness the California state fish, the bright orange garibaldi, swimming under your kayak in La Jolla Cove. With Everyday California you'll paddle from La Jolla Shores into one of the seven sea caves (conditions permitting) and then "surf" your kayak back to the beach. During the summer months, you'll encounter one of the world's largest schools of leopard sharks congregating in the warm shallow water of the cove. The four- to five-foot sharks are harmless to humans, and you may find yourself swimming with dozens of the docile creatures. Alternately, in winter months Everyday California takes kayakers two miles offshore to observe gray whales on their annual migration from Alaska to Baja California.

2261 Avenida de la Playa, 858-454-6195
everydaycalifornia.com
Neighborhood: La Jolla Shores

PLAY ONE OF AMERICA'S FINEST GOLF COURSES
AT TORREY PINES

The municipal Torrey Pines Golf Course sits adjacent to a state preserve on bluffs overlooking the sparkling Pacific Ocean—one of the world's most picturesque golf settings. The 36-hole paradise was built in 1957, and for more than fifty years it has been included in the PGA Tour. In 2008 Torrey Pines hosted one of the most dramatic US Opens, when Tiger Woods defeated Rocco Mediate during a sudden-death playoff. While the North Course is spectacular, the South Course is more challenging and has more sea-facing play. Although the course is open to the public, securing a tee time is tough. Reservations within seven days or fewer are available to residents only, but it's worth the effort. The facilities include a driving range, practice putting greens, and one of the largest golf shops in the western US.

11480 N. Torrey Pines Rd., 877-581-7171
sandiego.gov/park-and-recreation/golf/torreypines
Neighborhood: Torrey Pines

OTHER NOTEWORTHY GOLF SAN DIEGO COURSES

The Crossings at Carlsbad
5800 The Crossings Dr., Carlsbad, 760-444-1800
thecrossingsatcarlsbad.com

Coronado Municipal Golf Course
2000 Visalia Row, Coronado, 619-522-2455
golfcoronado.com

The Grand Golf Club at Fairmont Grand Del Mar
5200 Grand Del Mar Way, 858-314-1930
fairmont.com/san-diego

Balboa Park Golf Course
2600 Golf Course Dr., South Park, 619-235-1184

Steele Canyon
3199 Stonefield Dr., Jamul, 619-441-6900
steelecanyon.com

LIFT YOUR SPIRITS WITH SPRING WILDFLOWERS
IN THE ANZA-BORREGO DESERT

Each spring, arid Anza-Borrego Desert State Park blooms with a feast of color and fragrance as the annual wildflower show arrives for a short, sometimes spectacular display. The state park, two hours east of San Diego, is the largest in California. Its 600,000 acres include palm oases, slot canyons, rugged mountains, colorful badlands, and 110 miles of hiking trails. Amid this austere beauty, the quantity and diversity of the annual bloom depends on a cool winter and solid rainfall. Once or twice a decade, conditions align and a "super bloom" comes along to flood Instagram screens with vast carpets of yellow, purple, and pink wildflowers. Small patches typically start to appear in February, but the peak of the show—which might last only a week or two—usually falls in March. Make Mother Nature proud by sticking to the marked trails and *don't pick the flowers*!

200 Palm Canyon Dr., Borrego Springs, 760-767-4684
parks.ca.gov
Neighborhood: East San Diego County

STROLL THE OCEANSIDE PIER

Spend a day in Oceanside, San Diego County's third-largest community, easily reached from downtown in an hour via frequent Amtrak or Coaster service. It's a half-mile walk from the station down to Oceanside Pier, one of the longest wooden piers on the West Coast. Hundreds of fishermen line the pier every morning to compete with pelicans and harbor seals for the abundant fish swimming between the submerged pillars. Trek all the way to the end, almost two thousand feet, and grab a bite at Ruby's, a '50s-style burger-and-shake joint. Oceanside's beachfront extends for three miles and is home to international surfing competitions, endurance events, and outrigger races. But if you feel like getting in on some action, you can rent a bike, take out a kayak or paddle board, and get in on a beach volleyball game.

North Pacific St., 800-350-7873
visitoceanside.org
Neighborhood: Oceanside

MEANDER ALONG COASTAL ROCKS AND DISCOVER THE TIDE POOLS

San Diego boasts about seventy miles of beachfront and a number of rocky coastal stretches that invite us to observe the intertidal ecosystems where the land greets the sea. At low tide, when the seawater recedes, pockets and channels in the rock fill with small pools inhabited by a variety of creatures. One of the best spots is Point Loma's sandstone cliffs, below the Cabrillo Lighthouse. Barnacles and mussels abound, but keep an eye out for starfish, shore crabs, anemones, California sea hares, lobsters, and even the dark red Pacific octopus. If you're lucky, the vivid nudibranchs (sea slugs that look like tiny versions of creatures from a Star Wars bar scene) can be a spectacular sighting. Other great locations include the Ocean Beach Pier, Tourmaline Surf Park, La Jolla cliffs between the children's pool and the cove, and South Cardiff State Beach. November through March are optimal for tide pooling since the tide is low during daylight hours.

Neighborhood: coastal locations throughout San Diego

TIP

Be sure to check the daily tide report and note that collecting organisms at tide pools is strictly prohibited. Wear footwear with good grip that you don't mind getting wet (a change of clothes and shoes is also nice to have).

TAKE FLIGHT
IN A HOT AIR BALLOON

Floating silently across the rolling countryside is a fantasy for many of us, and the northern part of the county offers two options for flights in a hot air balloon. Liftoffs happen at dawn in Temecula Valley an hour north of downtown, passing over rural country scenes of rambling ranch houses, citrus trees, and vineyards, where in winter, snow-topped mountains serve as a backdrop. Or take off on a Champagne flight just before dusk along the Cardiff coastline, thirty minutes from downtown, and survey the farms and posh estates of Rancho Santa Fe and Carmel Valley as the breeze carries you gently inland. With Compass Balloons, the exact takeoff location is determined the day before based on winds and other conditions, and a maximum of eight passengers are aboard group flights. Private charters are available.

969 Villa Cardiff Dr., Cardiff, 760-292-3163
34225 Rancho California Rd., Temecula, 760-292-3163
compassballoons.com

TIP

Dedicated and dilettante balloonatics
alike congregate for the annual Temecula
Balloon & Wine Festival, held on a weekend
around June 1. Concerts, wine tastings,
and—of course—mass balloon launches
(and rides) are part of the festivities.

951-676-6713, tvbwf.com

ANGLE FOR A BITE
ON A SPORTFISHING TRIP

Once known as the "tuna capital of the world," San Diego is also one of the birthplaces of modern saltwater sportfishing. The harbor nurtures a massive sportfishing industry, with half- and full-day charters and overnight trips reaching fishing grounds up to a hundred miles offshore. On close-in trips, morning and afternoon departures target yellowtail, bass, barracuda, rockfish, bonito, and tuna, while multi-day journeys reach remote islands off Baja where yellowfin tuna and wahoo weighing over a hundred pounds are regularly taken. H&M Landing and Point Loma Sportsfishing handle scheduled and chartered trips on a variety of different boats equipped with state-of-the-art fish-finders. They'll rent tackle and gear, set you up with a California fishing license or Mexican permit, and will refer you to processing services to have your catch processed and frozen in convenient fillets.

Point Loma Sportfishing
1403 Scott St., 619-223-1627, pointlomasportfishing.com

H&M Landing
2803 Emerson St., 619-222-1144, hmlanding.com

Neighborhood: Point Loma

TACKLE THE
FIVE-PEAK CHALLENGE
AT MISSION TRAILS

Whether you stroll, pedal, or climb in it, eight-thousand-acre Mission Trails Regional Park, the sixth-largest municipally-owned park in the US, is a place to escape the freeway rat race, reconnect with San Diego's native landscapes, and more. This beautiful recreational area inside the city (twelve miles from downtown) encompasses rugged hills, a splendid canyon, and the slender San Diego River. There are sixty miles of trails and five peaks, including 1,592-foot Cowles Mountain, the highest point in the city. You'll get fine views from the top, a five-mile roundtrip hike from Big Rock—but why stop there? Park rangers encourage residents and visitors alike to ascend all five peaks, whether in a day (14.5 miles) or over five visits, and then these intrepid hikers can take home a pin for completing the challenge. The visitor center is worth checking out, with well-planned interpretive exhibits, four shows daily in a ninety-four-seat theatre, souvenirs, and ranger-led walks offered several times weekly.

1 Father Junipero Serra Trail, 619-668-3281
mtrp.org
Neighborhood: Mission Gorge

NAVIGATE THE MISSION BEACH BOARDWALK

Okay, so it's not a real boardwalk. Still, the concrete walkway paralleling the shoreline from Pacific Beach to Mission Beach is a great place to walk, jog, skate, rollerblade, cycle and people-watch across one of San Diego's most iconic scenes. I like biking it, navigating the steady procession of road hazards—dogs, strollers, surfboards—with the sun high overhead. The boardwalk can be crowded, especially on summer weekends, so plan on riding slowly. But that lazy, meandering pace means you'll soak up a lot of the cheery beach vibe, including a plethora of tattoos, piercings, and bronzed skin. There are a number of beach bars to stop at for liquid refreshment along the way. Bike rental shops are found from one end of Mission Boulevard to the other, but parking is easiest in the lots near Belmont Park.

Neighborhoods: Pacific Beach, Mission Beach

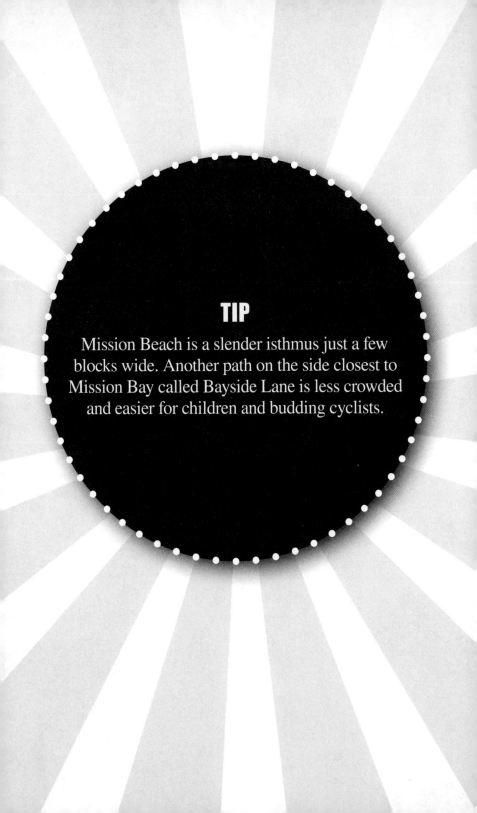

TIP

Mission Beach is a slender isthmus just a few blocks wide. Another path on the side closest to Mission Bay called Bayside Lane is less crowded and easier for children and budding cyclists.

Hotel del Coronado

CULTURE AND HISTORY

ABSORB THE VIEW
AT CABRILLO NATIONAL MONUMENT

San Diego's best viewpoint is revealed at this national monument
422 feet above sea level at the tip of Point Loma, the muscular peninsula
that dominates the entrance to San Diego Bay. You'll spot the hills
of Tijuana, nuclear submarines at Naval Base Point Loma, and—on
clear days—the mountainous backcountry that ruffles the horizon fifty
miles inland. In winter months gray whales can be spotted offshore,
and in spring wildflowers add drops of color. The breathtaking views
serve as a backdrop for the early history of San Diego, which began
when Portuguese explorer Juan Rodríguez Cabrillo discovered the
bay in 1542. A restored 1855 lighthouse illustrates the lonely life of
lightkeepers, and a small museum tells about gun batteries established
on the peninsula during WWII, when San Diego served as headquarters
for the Pacific Fleet.

1800 Cabrillo Memorial Dr., 619-523-4285
nps.gov/cabr
Neighborhood: Point Loma

APPRECIATE THE MASTERFUL ARCHITECTURE OF THE SALK INSTITUTE

After developing the polio vaccine, Jonas Salk sought to create a collaborative research environment. In 1960 the City of San Diego gifted Salk with twenty-seven prime acres overlooking the Pacific Ocean, and he partnered with architect Louis Kahn to design a research center "worthy of a visit by Picasso." The resulting Salk Institute is one of the most important architectural works in the US: austere structures of concrete, teak, lead, glass, and steel that provide open and unobstructed laboratory spaces to foster teamwork. A single, striking water feature unites the buildings, positioned so that the sun sets along its axis during the spring and fall equinoxes. Surprisingly few visitors seek out San Diego's architectural masterpiece, but it's an essential stop for anyone interested in modern design. Self-guided tours are available during weekday business hours and can be booked online.

10010 N. Torrey Pines Rd., 858-453-4100
salk.edu/about/visiting-salk
Neighborhood: Torrey Pines

EXPLORE THE MUSEUMS
OF BALBOA PARK

Even if one ignores the presence of the San Diego Zoo, Balboa Park represents one of the most vital urban cultural parks in the nation. Seventeen museums and cultural institutions cover a diverse range of subjects, from San Diego history to the development of flight, trains, and automobiles to the artistry of the old masters. And proving that the park's museums continue to grow and diversify, the Comic-Con Museum will open in 2021 to explore the world of comics and related popular arts. Don't overlook the park's architecture; structures with romantic, flamboyant Spanish-Renaissance façades were built along the Prado as part of the 1915 Panama-California Exposition. The Pan American Plaza, created for a subsequent 1935 exposition, showcases architectural styles ranging from Mexican pueblo to art deco. Save money by purchasing one of the multi-museum Balboa Park Explorer Passes valid for one, seven, or 365 days.

1549 El Prado, 619-239-0512
balboapark.org/explore/museums
Neighborhood: Uptown

TIP
Keep in mind that the zoo requires most of a day to tour, so you'll want to plan at least a second day in the park for the museums, gardens, and hiking trails.

TOP MUSEUMS OF BALBOA PARK

Fleet Science Center
1875 El Prado, 619-238-1233, rhfleet.org

Museum of Photographic Arts
1649 El Prado, 619-238-7559, mopa.org

San Diego Air & Space Museum
2001 Pan American Plaza, 619-234-8291
sandiegoairandspace.org

San Diego Automotive Museum
2080 Pan American Plaza, 619-231-2886
sdautomuseum.org

San Diego History Center
1649 El Prado, 619-232-6203, sandiegohistory.org

San Diego Model Railroad Museum
1649 El Prado, 619-696-0199, sdmrm.org

San Diego Museum of Man
1350 El Prado, 619-239-2001
museumofman.org

San Diego Natural History Museum
1788 El Prado, 877-946-7797, sdnhm.org

San Diego Museum of Art
1450 El Prado, 619-232-7931, sdmart.org

Timken Museum of Art
1500 El Prado, 619-239-5548, timkenmuseum.org

LET THE WAVES ROCK YOU TO SLEEP
AT CRYSTAL PIER HOTEL

Having trouble getting a good night's rest? You'll be lulled to sleep when you surf over to this cluster of cottages sitting literally right above the waves on Pacific Beach's vintage Crystal Pier. Each of the Cape Cod-style cottages sleeps two to six people and offers a living room, bedroom, fully equipped kitchen, and private patio with breathtaking ocean views. The sound of waves is soothing, and the pier sways gently with each passing swell. The whitewashed walls of these sweet, blue-shuttered cottages date to 1936, but all have been renovated. The boardwalk action is only a few steps (and worlds) away, and the views of sunsets and surfers are sublime. Guests can drive right out and park beside their cottages, a real boon on crowded weekends. The accommodations book up fast; it is necessary to reserve months in advance for summer and holiday weekends.

4500 Ocean Blvd., 800-748-5894 or 858-483-6983
crystalpier.com
Neighborhood: Pacific Beach

PROWL THE LEGENDARY HOTEL DEL CORONADO

"The Del," as it's affectionately known, is the epitome of a grand old seaside hotel and was built in 1888 on a sandy isle across from San Diego's then-young downtown. This national historic landmark—immortalized in the classic comedy *Some Like it Hot,* flaunts turn-of-the-century Victorian opulence, defined by red turrets, soaring cupolas, and gingerbread trim. Presidents, royalty, and celebrities have stayed at The Del over the years, and *Wizard of Oz* author L. Frank Baum so loved the resort that its architecture inspired cover artwork for the Oz series. Often packed to its rafters with tourists and wedding parties, guests pay an arm and a leg to bunk here. You can explore most of the public areas independently, but if you want a more in-depth look at the history of this iconic landmark, there are ninety-minute guided tours daily at 10:00 a.m. (and on weekends at 2:00 p.m.). There's also a Haunted Tour nightly at 7:00 p.m. with stories of the Del's notorious phantom Kate Morgan.

1500 Orange Ave., 619-522-8100
hoteldel.com
Neighborhood: Coronado

COMMUNE WITH PINNIPEDS
AT THE CHILDREN'S POOL

If you thought politics in Washington, DC were divisive, wait till you get a load of the backstory at the Children's Pool, arguably the most contentious piece of real estate in tony La Jolla. The jetty-protected cove was created in 1932 to provide a safe harbor for young children to swim. But since the 1990s, harbor seals have adopted this choice setting, using it as a rookery for their pups. From mid-December to mid-May the beach is closed to humans, when as many as two hundred seals can be viewed lazing in the sun and taking short dips in the sea. The community is sharply divided over retaking the beach for the diaper-clad set, but courts have sided with the easy-going seals. Meanwhile, it's an accessible glimpse into San Diego's marine ecology, with docents from the Sierra Club providing useful insight.

850 Coast Blvd.
sealconservancy.org
Neighborhood: La Jolla

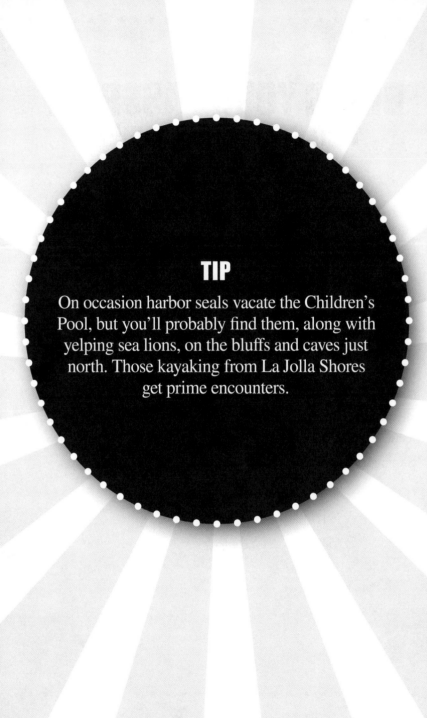

TIP

On occasion harbor seals vacate the Children's Pool, but you'll probably find them, along with yelping sea lions, on the bluffs and caves just north. Those kayaking from La Jolla Shores get prime encounters.

BRING YOUR PASSPORT
TO TASTE THE REAL TIJUANA
WITH TURISTA LIBRE

Since 2009, Derrik Chinn, a former journalist for the *San Diego Union-Tribune*, has been leading weekend day tours of beautifully bizarre Tijuana, the dynamic border city he now calls home. After meeting at the San Ysidro border crossing (the last stop on the San Diego Trolley line), groups embark on a guided tour based on one of several themes, each designed to help us discover Mexico's fourth largest city and feel less like outsiders and more like insiders. Popular tours include the craft brewery and taco hop; the "Meals of Migrants" food tour; and the market and street eats trek—each of them sidestepping stereotypes and clichés while embracing Mexico's rich and often beguiling heritage. Allow a full day for the six- to eight-hour tour, as border crossing times coming back are unpredictable. Private tours are also available.

turistalibre.com

FERRY TO BEAUTIFUL CORONADO ISLAND

Although Coronado is more of a peninsula connected by a narrow sand-spit, it does indeed have an island resort ambience, and it's a swell day trip by ferry from San Diego, just across the bay. The ferry service departs from two downtown locations: every thirty minutes from the foot of Fifth Avenue (behind the convention center), or hourly from the Broadway Pier next to the USS *Midway*. The ten-minute crossing deposits you at the Coronado Ferry Landing, where you'll find restaurants, shops, art galleries, free weekend concerts, and a farmers market on Tuesdays. Or rent a bike or surrey and cycle over to Orange Avenue, Coronado's charming downtown, and on to the historic Hotel del Coronado 1.5 miles away. The glorious beach fronting the hotel is one of San Diego's finest and extends south to the Silver Strand.

600 Convention Way, 619-234-4111
90 N. Harbor Dr., 619-234-4111
coronadoferrylanding.com
Neighborhoods: Coronado

Botanical Building and
Lily Pond, Balboa Park

FIND YOUR ZEN
IN THE GARDENS OF BALBOA PARK

The development of Balboa Park's extensive, mature botanical collection is thanks largely to Kate Sessions, a horticulturalist who was devoted to transforming the park's desolate mesas and scrub-filled canyons. In addition to the lush gardens inside the San Diego Zoo, stop by the much-photographed lily pond and botanical building built for the 1915 Exposition. Inside, the collection includes cycads, ferns, orchids, carnivorous plants, and tropical palms. Across Park Boulevard (past the Natural History Museum) lies the Desert Garden, containing more than 1,300 cacti, succulents, and drought-resistant plants (peak blooms January through March). Immediately next door is the Inez Grant Parker Memorial Rose Garden, with 1,600 rose bushes covering more than 130 varieties, with blooms peaking in April and May. The twelve-acre Japanese Friendship Garden requires a separate admission fee, but features centuries-old gardening techniques adapted to San Diego's climate, along with stone arrangements, koi ponds, and sukiya-style buildings. Whatever your particular botanical fancy, Balboa Park is a rewarding place to practice mindfulness in all its forms.

1549 El Prado, 619-239-0512
balboapark.org/explore/gardens
Neighborhood: Uptown

PICTURE ART ALIVE
AT THE SAN DIEGO MUSEUM OF ART

For one glorious spring weekend each year since 1982, the San Diego Museum of Art is transformed for its signature annual event, Art Alive, by a series of over a hundred living tableaux that reinterpret some of the museum's masterpieces in flowers—a union of paint and plant. The weekend starts with a major fundraiser, the Bloom Bash, a party where the floral interpretations are debuted, with their inspirations from the permanent collection—both sculptures and paintings—parked just behind. The interior rotunda is converted into a giant two-story sculpture of plants and flowers. A mix of the literal and the abstract, the whimsical and the contemplative, the April event is the museum's major fundraiser for the year and draws up to twelve thousand visitors over three days before being taken down on Sunday evening.

1450 El Prado, 619-232-7931
sdmart.org
Neighborhood: Balboa Park

APPLAUD THE BARD
AT THE OLD GLOBE THEATRE

One of the country's leading professional regional theatres is the Tony-winning Old Globe, a complex of three performance venues inside Balboa Park. Though best known for the 580-seat Old Globe—fashioned after Shakespeare's Globe Theatre in London—there are also the 250-seat Sheryl and Harvey White Theatre and the 620-seat open-air Lowell Davies Festival Theatre, used to stage rewarding summer Shakespeare performances under the stars. The Globe mounts fifteen productions each year, from world premieres of Broadway hits like *The Full Monty* and *Into the Woods* to the Christmas perennial, *Dr. Seuss's How the Grinch Stole Christmas!*, a popular family draw during the holidays since 1997. Note that parking is not adjacent to the Globe—allow an hour to locate parking and walk to the theatres.

1363 Old Globe Way, 619-234–5623
theoldglobe.org
Neighborhood: Balboa Park

DAYTRIP TO PALOMAR OBSERVATORY

Situated at an elevation of 5,598 feet atop Palomar Mountain, the highest point in San Diego County, this observatory was for several decades the world's largest telescope. It was funded by a $6 million grant from Caltech in 1928, but it took two decades—following trial-and-error fabrication of the 200-inch reflecting mirror in Corning, New York—before the Hale Telescope was finally ready to survey the skies. Many discoveries have been made, and researchers continue to study near-Earth asteroids, outer solar-system planets, star formations, black holes, quasars, and much more. The 135-foot-high dome containing the telescope is a beautifully understated Art Deco structure, with balanced proportions that dominate the surrounding forest. Located sixty-five miles from downtown, the observatory offers weekend guided tours from April through November, though booking a tour isn't necessary to visit. Check the forecast before visiting, especially in winter months.

35899 Canfield Rd., 760-742-2119, astro.caltech.edu/palomar
Neighborhood: Palomar Mountain

TIP
The quirky, mountain community of Palomar nearby has a campground, grocery store, restaurant, and post office.

CLAMBER DOWN
TO LA JOLLA'S SUNNY JIM SEA CAVE

Perched on bluffs just east of La Jolla Cove, the Cave Store shelters a secret passageway: a constricted, eerie tunnel descends from the store down 144 steps to a wood-plank observation deck opening onto the sea. The tunnel to the cave was hand-carved by two laborers in 1903 using picks and shovels, creating an early tourist attraction for the community. Sunny Jim is one of seven sea caves otherwise accessed only by kayak (or long swim). The cave got its name years later, when L. Frank Baum, author of *The Wizard of Oz*, said the cave's opening looked like a British cereal mascot named Sunny Jim. Over time, the cave was also used by smugglers who would bring ashore alcohol and illegal immigrants. Kids love this spooky experience—hold the handrail and your little ones' hands tightly.

1325 Coast Blvd., 858-459-0746
cavestore.com
Neighborhood: La Jolla

USS *Midway*

REDISCOVER AMERICAN NAVAL HISTORY ABOARD USS *MIDWAY*

In 2004, following half a century of service that began one week after the Japanese surrender in WWII, the USS *Midway* made her final voyage into San Diego Bay. By the time the aircraft carrier was decommissioned in 1992, *Midway* had served in the Vietnam War, operated as the flagship for Desert Storm, and evacuated 1,800 people from Subic Bay Naval Base in the Philippines when it was threatened by a volcano eruption. In all, more than 200,000 men served aboard the aircraft carrier, which was for ten years the largest vessel at sea. Today, *Midway* is a fascinating naval museum drawing more than 1.3 million visitors annually. A self-guided audio tour takes visitors to several levels of the *Midway*, telling the story of life on board, but the highlight is climbing the superstructure to the bridge and gazing down on the 1,001-foot-long flight deck, with various aircraft poised for duty.

910 N. Harbor Dr., 619-544-9600
midway.org
Neighborhood: Downtown

DISCOVER
THE BIRTHPLACE OF
SAN DIEGO IN OLD TOWN

San Diego was home to the original European settlement on the West Coast, where Franciscan Father Junípero Serra established San Diego de Alcalá, the first of twenty-one California missions. The small settlement situated below the mission is where the community began in the early 1800s. Old Town San Diego State Historic Park has been restored to highlight life in early California, particularly the Mexican-American period between 1821 and 1872. You'll find a schoolhouse, blacksmith's shop, newspaper office, stables, and more, all surrounding a central plaza. Free walking tours are offered daily at 11:00 a.m. and 2:00 p.m. There are restaurants and strolling mariachi bands at Fiesta de Reyes, a charming shopping complex inhabiting a former 1930s-era motel built in the adobe style, and many more Mexican eateries and shops can be found outside the park along San Diego Avenue.

4002 Wallace St., 619-220-5422
oldtownsandiego.org
Neighborhood: Old Town

CATCH A FUTURE TONY WINNER
AT LA JOLLA PLAYHOUSE

With more than 150 stages, San Diego is a premiere destination for theatre, sending more shows to Broadway than any other city in America. Many of them originate at the La Jolla Playhouse, internationally celebrated for creating some of the most exciting work in American theatre. The playhouse boasts a Hollywood pedigree—it was founded in 1947 by Gregory Peck, Dorothy McGuire, and Mel Ferrer—but it regularly sends shows to Broadway, and they return home clutching Tony Awards. Thirty-two of these statues have been earned to date, for such long-running hits as *Come From Away*, *Jersey Boys*, and The Who's *Tommy*. Situated on the campus of the University of California, San Diego, the playhouse runs four venues, the principal one being the 492-seat, proscenium-style Mandell Weiss Theatre.

2910 La Jolla Village Dr., 858-550-1070
lajollaplayhouse.org
Neighborhood: La Jolla

Maritime Museum of San Diego

MASTER NAUTICAL HISTORY
AT THE MARITIME MUSEUM OF SAN DIEGO

As befits one of America's great sailing harbors, San Diego is home to a world-class maritime museum with a collection of historic vessels. The fleet, docked at the Embarcadero, includes the HMS *Surprise* (featured in the Oscar-winning film *Master and Commander*), the 1898 steam ferry *Berkeley*, and Soviet-era Russian submarine *B-39*. The star of the show is the world's oldest active ship, *Star of India*, dating to 1863 and newly refurbished in 2020. There are rewarding exhibits on board each vessel offering hands-on, family-friendly experiences. Better yet, sign up for a four-hour circuit of San Diego Bay aboard the historic small vessel *Californian*, a replica of a gold rush-era cutter and the official tall ship of the State of California, or aboard the *San Salvador*, a replica of Cabrillo's ship that arrived in the bay in 1542.

1492 N Harbor Dr., 619-234-9153
sdmaritime.org
Neighborhood: Downtown

SKETCH YOURSELF INTO THE SCENE
AT COMIC-CON

Every year, for one long July weekend, San Diego becomes the center of the comics-lover's universe. Since 1970, when the very first Comic-Con convention was organized, the nonprofit event has grown to draw 135,000 attendees to the San Diego Convention Center—and sells out *eight* months in advance! Luring comic book fans, sci-fi geeks, cosplayers, pop culture buffs, and bystanders alike, the event has becine a multimedia sensation that incorporates all genres of collectibles, toys, and games. Even from the sidelines, Comic-Con is a people-watching bonanza, where enthusiasts dressed in wild costumes can parade in a judgement-free universe. A substantial Hollywood contingent also comes to launch the latest fantasy, horror, sci-fi, and animated products—the sneak previews of movies and TV shows headed to the screen alike are often attended by some of the biggest celebrities.

111 W. Harbor Dr., 619-491-2475
comic-con.org
Neighborhood: Downtown

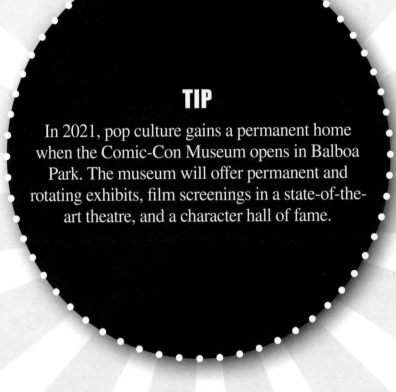

TIP

In 2021, pop culture gains a permanent home when the Comic-Con Museum opens in Balboa Park. The museum will offer permanent and rotating exhibits, film screenings in a state-of-the-art theatre, and a character hall of fame.

PAY TRIBUTE TO MISSION BASILICA SAN DIEGO DE ALCALÁ

Originally established above Old Town, this was the first link in what became a chain of twenty-one California missions. They were founded by Father Junípero Serra, a Spanish priest charged with spreading Christianity among the native inhabitants of the New World. In 1774, the mission was moved to its present site just up the valley, where agricultural prospects were better, on a rise that offered views of the surrounding marshes, plains, and mesas. A dam built just upriver was probably the first irrigation project in the West, allowing Serra's flock to grow wheat, barley, vineyards, olives, and dates. Also noteworthy: in using adobe for walls and clay tile roofs, Father Serra inspired a long list of twentieth-century architects to adopt the same style for structures throughout California. You can worship at the birthplace of Christianity on the West Coast; Mass is held daily for the active parish.

10818 San Diego Mission Rd., 619-283-7319
missionsandiego.org
Neighborhood: Mission Valley

TIP

Other missions near San Diego include Mission San Antonia de Pala near Mount Palomar, and Mission Santa Ysabel near Julian. Known as "the King of Missions," Mission San Luis Rey de Francia in Oceanside is the largest of California's missions and one of its most beautiful.

PICNIC WITH A FREE OUTDOOR CONCERT
AT THE SPRECKELS ORGAN PAVILION

Donated to the citizens of San Diego in 1914 by brothers John D. and Adolph Spreckels, this ornate, curved pavilion houses a magnificent organ with 4,518 individual pipes—it's the largest outdoor organ in the world. The pipes range from the size of a pencil to more than thirty-two feet long. With only brief interruptions, the organ has been in continuous use for over a century, and today you can enjoy free hour-long concerts on Sundays at 2:00 p.m., rain or shine, given by San Diego Civic Organist Raúl Prieto Ramírez. Additional concerts are scheduled on Mondays at 7:30 p.m. from late June through the end of August and on other evenings throughout the year. There's seating for 2,400, but little shade, so bring an umbrella on warm days or on the rare drizzly afternoon.

El Prado, 619-702-8138
spreckelsorgan.org
Neighborhood: Balboa Park

FLOCK TO THE LIVING COAST DISCOVERY CENTER

Established to protect rare wildlife, the San Diego Bay National Wildlife Refuge encompasses much of the southern end of the bay, bordered on the east by Chula Vista. Although these intertidal mudflat and coastal salt marsh habitats are home to four endangered or threatened species, over two hundred total bird species have been observed at the marsh, an important wintering area for many shorebirds. The Living Coast Discovery Center is aimed at guests of all ages, inviting us to explore the region's flora and fauna. The nonprofit zoo and aquarium offers hands-on exhibits and up-close encounters with plant and animal species native to Southern California coastal habitats, and there are daily feeding presentations with endangered green sea turtles, stingrays, leopard sharks, and American bald and golden eagles. The center's large collection of raptors also includes hawks, falcons, owls, an American bald eagle, a golden eagle, and more.

1000 Gunpowder Point Dr., 619-409-5900
thelivingcoast.org
Neighborhood: Chula Vista

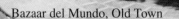
Bazaar del Mundo, Old Town

SHOPPING AND FASHION

BROWSE WITH TIJUANEROS
AT LAS AMERICAS PREMIUM OUTLETS

San Diego's largest outlet mall, Las Americas is more than the sum of its hundred-plus stores. The mall sits twenty minutes south of downtown, literally a stone's throw from the border crossing into Tijuana, Mexico. As such, the mall attracts a diverse crowd from both sides of *la frontera*, all in search of bargains from the name brands hanging their outlet flags: Ann Taylor, Armani, Disney, Hugo Boss, Michael Kors, North Face, Polo, and Tommy Hilfiger, just to name a few. It's an oddly positive cultural experience at the convergence of the two countries, with "The Wall" looming just a hundred feet away. The nearby Achiote Restaurant offers authentic Mexican breakfast, lunch, and dinner (try the *chilaquiles*). Las Americas is easily reached via the San Diego Trolley—the San Ysidro stop is just a ten-minute walk from the entrance.

4211 Camino de la Plaza, San Ysidro, 619-934-8400
premiumoutlets.com/outlet/las-americas
Neighborhood: San Diego-Tijuana border crossing

TIP

Carlsbad Premium Outlets, forty minutes north of downtown, is the other major outlet mall for the San Diego area. Brands worth seeking out include Crate & Barrel, Le Creuset, Robert Graham, Tory Burch, True Religion, and Tumi.

TRY ON YOUR DESIGNER INSTINCTS
ALONG CEDROS AVENUE

An eclectic mélange of nearly a hundred indie shops, boutiques, and galleries packed into a few short blocks, the Cedros Avenue Design District is a treasure trove of designer goods. Some of the vendors are housed in a row of Quonset huts that were constructed in the 1950s for a defense contractor who made spy plane photographic equipment and other gear. Today, more than two dozen chic stores sell furniture, original art, photographs, home decor, and clothing on that very site. Lotus is a fourteen-thousand-square-foot collective representing dozens of local artisans and designers, with a healthy focus on products that are fair trade and ethically sourced. There are cafés, a brewery, an olive oil purveyor, and on Sundays, a farmers market blossoms from noon to 4:00 p.m. Bonus: the Coaster station is next door, making Cedros Avenue an easy trip from downtown.

S. Cedros Ave., Solana Beach, 858-755-0444
cedrosavenue.com
Neighborhood: Solana Beach

BRUSH SHOULDERS WITH FAMED AUTHORS
AT WARWICK'S

Other cities may have bigger, more trendy, or more niche options for stocking bookshelves, but Warwick's is the oldest family-owned and continuously operated bookstore in the United States. Founded in 1896, this La Jolla institution has a knowledgeable staff that stays abreast of local authors, and its roots in the local community go deep. Over the years, Warwick's has hosted countless world-class writers on book tours, such as Barbara Kingsolver, Isabelle Allende, Kirk Douglas, David Sedaris, Alice Walker, Hillary Clinton, and Margaret Thatcher—from presidents and senators to Pulitzer Prize winners and celebrities, they've all been here. But even when a bestselling author isn't in the house, count on about twenty-five thousand titles to peruse and purchase. In addition to books you'll find Warwick's to be San Diego's best stationery store, with choice office supplies and other gifts readily available.

7812 Girard Ave., 858-454-0347
warwicks.com
Neighborhood: La Jolla

BUY ORIGINAL ART
AT SPANISH VILLAGE ART CENTER

Occupying a cluster of thirty-six low-slung, ramshackle bungalows just south of the San Diego Zoo, the Spanish Village Art Center is a working-artists' collective. The charming buildings were meant to be temporary, housing restaurants and shops for the 1935-36 expo. But just before demolition, local artists approached the city and proposed to convert the village into working art studios and to provide community outreach. The artists gained an affordable place to work and sell their art, and they frequently open their studio doors to the public, providing opportunities to watch the creative process. The artists—more than two hundred—come from a variety of backgrounds and places, and include award-winning painters, sculptors, metalsmiths, photographers, printmakers, and jewelry designers who work with clay, gourds, fiber, mixed media, glass, enamel, and leather, among other things. Artists can be found creating beautiful pieces in their Village studios on any given day, but the center really hums with activity on weekends.

1770 Village Place, 619 233-9050
spanishvillageart.com
Neighborhood: Balboa Park

SURRENDER TO YOUR SHOPPING HABIT
AT WESTFIELD UTC

Okay, so "UTC"—formerly University Towne Centre—isn't the sexiest name, but this large outdoor shopping center completed a major renovation and expansion in 2020 to stand today as San Diego's swankiest mall. UTC epitomizes California living, and with more than 150 stores plus dozens of other services, it has become a centerpiece of consumerism in the greater La Jolla area. Anchor stores include Macy's and Nordstrom, while venues such as Hermès, Crate & Barrel, Tesla, and Aesop draw more discerning types. There's an ice-skating rink, multilevel 24-Hour Fitness, and the ArcLight Cinema with fourteen screens and stadium-style seating. Dining is a big attraction, at a variety of price points, with places like Din Tai Fung (Taiwan soup dumplings), Napizza (Roman-style square pies), and Larsen's (steaks) keeping visitors sated and happy well into the evening.

4545 La Jolla Village Dr., 858-546-8858
westfield.com
Neighborhood: La Jolla

SHOP SOUTH OF THE BORDER WITHOUT A PASSPORT
AT BAZAAR DEL MUNDO

Tijuana is just a twenty-minute drive from downtown San Diego. But why fight border traffic on the return when you can take in south-of-the-border-style shopping at Bazaar del Mundo? This meticulously curated collection of boutiques offers an array of kitchenware, vivid tablecloths, hand-blown glassware, and Talavera dishes. Shoppers can find party goods like artisan-crafted piñatas, ornaments, toys and dolls, along with festive Mexican folk art, Guatemalan textiles, Mata Ortiz pottery, and Navajo jewelry. Although you won't find the bargain prices available on the other side of the border, the goods are generally of higher quality. There isn't a more colorful place to browse in San Diego, and if you get hungry, wander next door for tacos and tamales at Casa Guadalajara.

4133 Taylor St., 619-296-3161
bazaardelmundo.com
Neighborhood: Old Town

TIP

As an alternative, Artelexia embraces an upcycling aesthetic by cleverly repurposing frugal Mexican products to create items of cheerful beauty, such as handmade shadow boxes known as *nichos*. Much of the artwork is sourced from Oaxaca—feel free to explore with a *paleta* (popsicle) in hand.

3803 Ray St.; 619-501-6381
artelexia.com
Neighborhood: North Park

EMBARK ON A RETAIL THERAPY JOURNEY
IN MISSION VALLEY

Consumer central for San Diegans is Mission Valley. For one mile on either side of the slender San Diego River, two of the city's biggest outdoor malls provide nearly three million square feet of retail space. Mission Valley is the older of the two, hosting stores aimed at bargain-hunters such as Bed, Bath & Beyond, Bloomingdale's Outlet, and Nordstrom Rack. You'll also find Target, Macy's Home, a twenty-screen AMC movie theatre, and more than a hundred other stores and places to eat. Across the streets to the north and west are separate complexes featuring additional stores. The more upscale Fashion Valley has six anchor tenants: JCPenney, Macy's, Neiman Marcus, Nordstrom, Bloomingdale's, and Forever 21, plus high-end stores like Prada, Apple, Gucci, and two hundred others. There are several solid restaurants and another eighteen-screen AMC theatre, plus smaller malls just east of Highway 163.

Mission Valley: 1640 Camino Del Rio N., San Diego, 619-296-6375
westfield.com/missionvalley

Fashion Valley: 7007 Friars Rd., San Diego, 619-297-3381
simon.com/mall/fashion-valley Neighborhood: Mission Valley

TIP

Both shopping centers are easily accessible via San Diego Trolley. Take the Green Line from downtown, Old Town, or East County. The malls are just a two-minute walk from their respective stops on the Green Line.

LOSE YOURSELF
IN THE BOUTIQUES OF LA JOLLA

Nicknamed "The Jewel," the village of La Jolla is ideal for shoppers as well as strolling couples, people-watchers, and anyone who enjoys sea air and glimpses of crashing waves. You'll find name brands like Kate Spade, Talbots, and Lululemon Athletica, alongside one-of-a-kind boutiques ranging from haute couture to the comfortably familiar. The best shopping is concentrated along tony Prospect Street (which some refer to as San Diego's Rodeo Drive) and on three avenues abutting it: Ivanhoe, Herschel, and Girard. Look for fine jewelry, luxury watches, and estate pieces at CJ Charles; small designers, local artists, and ready-to-wear at Pomegranate; and "surfer chic meets bohemian gypsy goddess" at RICA Boutique. Throw in America's longest-running family-owned bookstore (Warwick's), art and artifacts from Africa and Beyond, San Diego's best toy store (Geppetto's), and some of San Diego's favorite restaurants, and you have a full day of retail R&R.

858-230-2725
lajollabythesea.com
Neighborhood: La Jolla

• •

SUGGESTED
ITINERARIES

ACTIVE OUTDOOR ADVENTURES

Honor the Undeveloped California Coastline at Torrey Pines, 66

Cycle the Bayshore Bikeway, 67

Dive Wreck Alley, 70

Look before You Leap at Torrey Pines Gliderport, 71

Hike Mt. Woodson (and Take a Bite of Potato Chip Rock), 75

Sail the America's Cup Racing Yacht, *Stars & Stripes,* 77

Learn How to Ride the Waves with a Surf Diva, 81

Paddle with Whales and Sea Lions and Sharks, Oh My!, 85

Play One of America's Finest Golf Courses at Torrey Pines, 86

Meander along Coastal Rocks and Discover the Tide Pools, 90

CULTURAL AFFAIRS

Cross the Border to Discover Mexico's Premiere Wine Region, 27

Bend Your Ear for Summer Pops at San Diego Symphony's Shell, 43

Appeciate the Masterful Architecture of the Salk Institute, 101

Explore the Museums of Balboa Park, 102

Bring Your Passport to Taste the Real Tijuana with Turista Libre, 108

Applaud the Bard at the Old Globe Theatre, 113

Catch a Future Tony Winner at La Jolla Playhouse, 119

Sketch Yourself into the Scene at Comic-Con, 122

Picnic with a Free Outdoor Concert at the Spreckels Organ Pavilion, 126

Buy Original Art at Spanish Village Art Center, 134

ESSENTIAL SAN DIEGO

Kiss the High Tide at the Marine Room, 6

Savor Mexico at Casa Guadalajara, 7

Go Local at the Hillcrest Farmers Market and Open-Air Bazaar, 24

Bend Your Ear for Summer Pops at San Diego Symphony's Shell, 43

Honor the Undeveloped California Coastline at Torrey Pines, 66

Look before You Leap at Torrey Pines Gliderport, 71

Strip to your Birthday Suit at Black's Beach, 73

Learn How to Ride the Waves with a Surf Diva, 81

Paddle with Whales and Sea Lions and Sharks, Oh My!, 85

Meander along Coastal Rocks and Discover the Tide Pools, 90

Commune with Pinnipeds at the Children's Pool, 106

Ferry to Beautiful Coronado Island, 109

FAMILY FUN

Pick Sweet, Vine-Ripened Fruit at Carlsbad Strawberry Company, 15

Roar and Snore with the Beasties at San Diego Zoo Safari Park, 46

Rejoice in Christmas at the San Diego Parade of Lights, 50

Kid Around at Legoland, 56

Skate by the Sea at the Hotel del Coronado, 74

Muss Your Hair and Rattle Your Bones on the Giant Dipper, 79

Learn How to Ride the Waves with a Surf Diva, 81

Paddle with Whales and Sea Lions and Sharks, Oh My!, 85

Meander along Coastal Rocks and Discover the Tide Pools, 90

Clamber Down to La Jolla's Sunny Jim Sea Cave, 115

FOOD FINDS

Eat the Farm at A. R. Valentien, 2

Slice Up a Mouth-Watering Pizza at Il Dandy, 12

Roll Up to the Bar for Omakase at Sushi Ota, 18

Satisfy Your Taco Cravings at ¡SALUD!, 20

Indulge in Extraordinary Desserts, 22
Go Local at the Hillcrest Farmers Market and Open-Air Bazaar, 24
Forage for Global Foods at Liberty Public Market, 28
Elevate Your Brunch Game at Morning Glory, 33
Relish the Royale—with Cheese, 34
Devour an Asian Feast on Convoy Street, 36

LIQUID LIBATIONS

Splurge on a Grammy-Winner's Java at Bird Rock Coffee Roasters, 8
Drink In the Sunset at Top of the Hyatt, 14
Quaff Craft Suds at Stone Brewing World Bistro, 16
Raise the Bar on Craft Cocktails at Raised by Wolves, 26
Celebrate the Local Suds during San Diego Beer Week, 32
Quench your Polynesian Fantasies with a Bali Hai Mai Tai, 37
Cross the Border to Discover Mexico's Premiere Wine Region, 27
Dance the Night Away at Omnia, 58

FREEBIES

Rejoice in Christmas at the San Diego Parade of Lights, 50
March for Independence Day and the Big Bay Boom, 62
Pamper Your Pooch at Dog Beach, 72
Amble along Sunset Cliffs for Dreamy Seaside Vistas, 82
Tackle the Five-Peak Challenge at Mission Trails, 95
Navigate the Mission Beach Boardwalk, 96
Commune with Pinnipeds at the Children's Pool, 106
Find Your Zen in the Gardens of Balboa Park, 111
Discover the Birthplace of San Diego in Old Town, 118
Picnic with a Free Outdoor Concert at the Spreckels Organ Pavilion, 126

HISTORY LESSONS

Sail the America's Cup Racing Yacht, *Stars & Stripes*, 77
Absorb the View at Cabrillo National Monument, 100

Prowl the Legendary Hotel del Coronado, 105
Rediscover American Naval History aboard USS Midway, 117
Daytrip to Palomar Observatory, 114
Discover the Birthplace of San Diego in Old Town, 118
Master Nautical History at the Maritime Museum of San Diego, 121
Pay Tribute to Mission Basilica San Diego de Alcalá, 124

ROMANTIC RENDEZVOUS

Eat the Farm at A. R. Valentien, 2
Stake Your Claim at Born and Raised, 4
Kiss the High Tide at the Marine Room, 6
Drink In Sunset at Top of the Hyatt, 14
Add a Star to Your Dining Priorities with Addison, 33
Amble along Sunset Cliffs for Dreamy Seaside Vistas, 82
Take Flight in a Hot Air Balloon, 92
Let the Waves Rock You to Sleep at Crystal Pier Hotel, 104

SPORTS SPOTS

Take Me Out to a Padres Game at Petco Park, 52
Revel in the Adult Antics of Over-the-Line, 59
Cycle the Bayshore Bikeway, 67
Dive Wreck Alley, 70
Learn How to Ride the Waves with a Surf Diva, 81
Play One of America's Finest Golf Courses at Torrey Pines, 86
Angle for a Bite on a Sportfishing Trip, 94
Tackle the Five-Peak Challenge at Mission Trails, 95

ACTIVITIES
BY SEASON

SPRING

Pick Sweet, Vine-Ripened Fruit at Carlsbad Strawberry Company, 15
Wander through the Flower Fields of Carlsbad, 61
Lift Your Spirits with Spring Wildflowers in the Anza-Borrego Desert, 88
Picture Art Alive at the San Diego Museum of Art, 112

SUMMER

Bend Your Ear for Summer Pops at San Diego Symphony's Shell, 43
Enjoy Top Touring Acts at Humphrey's by the Bay, 48
Take Me Out to a Padres Game at Petco Park, 52
Revel in the Adult Antics of Over-the-Line, 59
March for Independence Day and the Big Bay Boom, 62
Track Down a Deep-Fried Twinkie at the San Diego Fair, 80
Run with the Grunions, 78
Applaud the Bard at the Old Globe Theatre, 113
Sketch Yourself into the Scene at Comic-Con, 122

FALL

Celebrate the Local Suds during San Diego Beer Week, 32

WINTER

Rejoice in Christmas at the San Diego Parade of Light, 50
Sail Away to Distant Horizons from the Port of San Diego, 60
Rendezvous with Cetaceans on a Whale-Watching Tour, 68
Skate by the Sea at the Hotel del Coronado, 74

INDEX

Abbruzzino, Chef Antonio, 12
Addison, x, 3, 144
Albert's Restaurant, 45
Alpine Beer Company Pub, 17
Altitude Sky Lounge, 14
Ambrogio15 (restaurant), 13
America, The, 69
Anza-Borrego Desert State Park, 88
Art Alive, 112, 145
Artelexia, 137
A. R. Valentien, 2, 142, 142, 144
Asian food, 36
Automatic Brewing, 17
Balboa Park, 44, 52, 87, 102, 103, 111, 123, 141, 143
Balboa Park Golf Course, 87
Bali Hai, 37, 143
Ballast Point, 17
bakery, 10
Bankers Hill, 12, 22, 30, 31, 35
Bankers Hill Bar & Restaurant, 35
Barrio Logan, x, 20–21
Baum, L. Frank, 105, 115
Bayshore Bikeway, 67, 141, 144
Bazaar del Mundo, 136
Belly Up Tavern, 42
Belmont Park, 79, 96
Biga, 31
Big Bay Boom, 62–63, 143, 145
Birch Aquarium, 51
Bird Rock Coffee Roasters, 8, 143
Black's Beach, 71, 73, 142
Blind Lady Ale House, 17
Borkum, Tracy, 30
Born and Raised, 4, 144
Borrego Springs, 88
Bradley, Chef William, 3
Bread & Cie, 10
Bronx Pizza, 13
Bully's East Prime Bistro Sports Bar, 5
Buona Forchetta, 13
Burgers, 16
Cabrillo, Juan Rodríguez, 100
Cabrillo National Monument, 100, 143
C Level, 19
Caffè Calabria, 9
Cantina Mayahuel, 21
Cardiff, 90, 92
Caribbean, 60

Carlsbad, 15, 61, 87
Carlsbad Premium Outlets, 61, 131, 145
Carlsbad Strawberry Company, 15, 142, 145
Carmel Valley, 3, 8, 92
Carnival Cruises, 60
Casa Guadalajara, 7, 136, 142
Casbah, The, 53
casino, 55
Cedros Avenue Design District, 132
Chicano Park, 67
Children's Pool, 90, 106–107, 142, 143
Chinn, Derrik, 108
Christmas, 50, 74, 113, 142, 143, 145
Chula Vista, 67, 127
City Tacos, 21
Civico 1845, 31
Cliffhanger Café, 71
Coaster commuter rail, 42
cocktails, 26, 143
Conner, Dennis, 77
Convoy Street, 36, 143
Comic-Con, 102, 122, 123, 141, 145
Copley Symphony Hall, 43
Coronado, 14, 17, 25, 29, 50, 62–63, 67, 74, 78, 87, 105, 109, 142, 144, 145
Coronado Brewing, 17
Coronado Ferry Landing, 63, 109
Coronado Municipal Golf Course, 87
Cowboy Star Restaurant and Butcher Shop, 5
Cowles Mountain, 95
craft brewery, 16, 108
Crazee Burger, 35
Crossings at Carlsbad, The, 87
cruise lines, 29, 60, 68, 77
Crystal Pier Hotel, 104, 144
Cucina Urbana, 30
cycling, 67
Dark Horse Coffee Roasters, 9
Del Mar, 3, 80, 87
desert, x, 88, 111, 145
desserts, 14, 22, 23, 143
Disney Cruises, 60
Dog Beach, 72, 143
downtown (neighborhood), 5, 14, 29, 43, 52, 58, 60, 68, 117, 121, 122
drinks, 14, 53, 74
El Cajon, 49, 55
Embarcadero, 50, 63, 121
Escondido, 16, 25, 46

Everyday California, 85
Extraordinary Desserts, 22, 143
Fairmont Grand Del Mar, 3, 87
farmers market, 24, 25, 109, 132, 142, 143
Fashion Valley, 138
Fiesta de Reyes, 118
Fiesta Island, 59
fireworks, 62
fishing, 94, 144
Flagship Cruises, 29
Fleet Science Center, 103
Flower Fields, The, 61, 145
Galaxy Taco, 21
garibaldi, 51, 85
Gaslamp Quarter, 14, 58
George's Ocean Terrace, 39
Giant Dipper, 79, 142
Golden Hill, 5, 9
golf, 2–3, 56, 79, 86–87, 141, 144
drag, 49
Grand Golf Club at Fairmont Grand Del Mar,
    The, 87
grunions, 78, 145
Guadalupe Valley, 27
Guillas, Executive Chef Bernard, 6
H&M Landing, 94
Harbor Island, 5, 19, 50, 63
harbor seals, 89, 106–107
Hawaii, 8, 60
hiking, 88, 102
Hillcrest, 10, 24, 142–143
Hillcrest Farmers Market, 24, 142–143
Holland America Line, 60
Hornblower Cruises, 68
hot air balloon, 92
Hotel del Coronado, 67, 74, 105, 109, 142,
    144, 145
Humphrey's Concerts by the Bay, 48
ice-skating, 28, 135
Il Dandy, 12, 31, 142
Imperial Beach, 21, 25, 67
Independence Day, 62, 143, 145
Ironside, 11
Island Prime, 5, 19
Italian (food), 11, 31
Jackson, Chef Jeff, 2
Jamul, 87
Jayne's Gastropub, 35
Julian Pie Company, 23
June Gloom, 47
Kahn, Louis, 101
Karl Strauss Brewing Co., 17
Kearny Mesa, 36
Krasne, Pastry Chef Karen, 22

La Jolla, 24, 26, 35, 66, 73, 81, 83–85, 90,
    106–107, 115, 119, 140, 141, 142
La Jolla Ecological Reserve, 85
La Jolla Playhouse, 119, 141
La Jolla Shores, 73, 81, 107
La Mesa, 9, 21
Las Americas Premium Outlets, 130
Las Cuatro Milpas, 21
LEGOLAND California, 56–57, 142
Liberty Public Market, 28, 143
Liberty Station, 13, 16, 28
Lily Pond and Botanical Building, 111
Lindbergh, Charles, 71
Lips, 49
Little Italy, 4, 11, 30, 53
Living Coast Discovery Center, 127
Lodge Torrey Pines, The. See A. R.
    Valentien; Torrey Pines Golf Course
Manchester Grand Hyatt, 14
Marine Room, The, 6, 142, 144
Maritime Museum of San Diego, 121, 144
Marriott Gaslamp Quarter, 14
May Gray, 47
Mexican food, 7, 20, 27, 118
Mexican Riviera, 60
Michelin (award), 3, 12
Midtown, 35
Midway, USS, 109, 117, 144
Mission Basilica San Diego de Alcalá, 124,
    144
Mission Bay, 97
Mission Beach, 59, 70, 96–97, 143
Mission Gorge, 95
Mission Trails Regional Park, 95
Mission Valley, 138
Morning Glory, 33, 143
Mostra Coffee, 9
Mount Woodson, 75
Mraz, Jason, 8
Museum of Photographic Arts, 103
North Park, 9, 13, 21, 25, 31, 35, 49, 137
Observatory, The, 53
Ocean Beach, 72, 82, 90
Oceanside, 125
Oceanside Pier, 89
Old Globe Theatre, 113, 141, 145
Old Town, 21, 118, 124, 139, 143, 144
Old Town San Diego State Historic Park, 118
OMNIA, 58, 143
Ota, Chef Yukito, 18, 142
Over-the-Line, 59, 144, 145
Pacific Beach, 81, 96, 104
Palomar Observatory, 114, 144
Panama-California Exposition, 102

Panama Canal, 60
pasta, 12, 30
Petco Park, 14, 52, 144, 145
Piacere Mio, 31
picnic, 126, 141, 143
pizza, 12–13, 17, 30, 52, 142
Pizza Port, 17
Point Loma, 16, 68, 70, 82, 90, 94, 100
Point Loma Sportfishing, 94
Potato Chip Rock, 75, 141
Poway, 75
Public House La Jolla, 35
Puesto, 21
Pummarò Pizzeria, 13
Rare Society, 5
Raised by Wolves, 26, 143
Royale, 34, 143
Rubio, Ralph, 39
Rubio's Coastal Grill, 39
sailing, 29, 69, 77, 121
Salk Institute, 101, 141
¡SALUD!, 20, 142
San Diego Air & Space Museum, 103
San Diego Automotive Museum, 103
San Diego Bay, 14, 19, 29, 37, 43, 50, 63, 67, 77, 100, 117, 121, 127
San Diego Beer Week, 32, 143, 145
San Diego de Alcalá, *See* Mission San Diego de Alcalá
San Diego Convention Center, 122
San Diego County Fair, 80
San Diego History Center, 103
San Diego Model Railroad Museum, 103
San Diego Museum of Art, 103, 112, 145
San Diego Museum of Man, 103
San Diego Natural History Museum, 103
San Diego Padres, 52
San Diego Parade of Lights, 50, 142, 143
San Diego Symphony, x, 43, 141, 142
San Diego Trolley, 67, 108, 130, 139
San Diego Zoo, 44–46, 102, 111, 134, 142
San Diego Zoo Safari Park, 45, 46, 142
San Pasqual Valley, 46
Scripps Institution of Oceanography, 51
Seafood, 11, 28, 29
Sea Life Aquarium, 56
sea lions, 85, 107, 141, 142
Seaport Village, 50, 63
SeaWorld San Diego, 54
Serra, Father Junípero, 118, 124
Sessions, Kate, 111
sharks, 51, 54, 85, 127, 141, 142
Shell, The, 43, 141, 142, 145
Shelter Island, 37, 48, 50, 63, 77

Siamo Napoli, 13, 31
Silver Strand, 67, 78, 81, 109
Smothers, Liz, 23
Solana Beach, 42
Sorrento Mesa, 17
South Park, x, 13, 31, 87
Spanish Village Art Center, 134, 141
Spreckels Organ Pavilion, 126, 141, 143
Starlite, 35
Stars & Stripes (USA-11), 77, 141, 143
steakhouse, 4–5, 19, 55
Steele Canyon, 87
Stone Brewing World Bistro, 16, 143
Sunny Jim Sea Cave, 115, 142
Sunset Cliffs, 82, 143, 144
Surf Diva Surf School, 81, 141, 142, 144
surfing, 89
sushi, 18, 142
Sushi Ota, 18, 142
Sycuan, 55
tacos, 11, 16, 20–21, 37, 39, 52, 108, 136
Temecula Wine Country, 27
tide pools, 51, 90–91, 141, 142
Tijuana, 14, 20, 27, 67, 70, 100, 108, 130, 136, 141
Timken Museum of Art, 103
Top of the Hyatt, 14, 143, 144
Torrey Pines, 2, 8, 66–67, 71, 73, 86, 101, 141, 142, 144
Torrey Pines Gliderport, 71, 73, 145, 144
Torrey Pines Golf Course, 86
Torrey Pines State Natural Reserve, 66
Tourmaline Park, 81, 90
Tribute Pizza, 13
Turf Supper Club, 5
Turista Libre, 108, 141
University Heights, 5
University of California, San Diego (UCSD), 119
Warwick's, 133, 140
Wegeforth, Dr. Harry, 45
WestBean Coffee Roasters, 9
Westfield UTC, 26, 145
whales, 54, 68–69, 85, 100, 141, 142
Wheel Fun Rentals, 67
wildflowers, 66, 88, 100, 145
Wild Note Café, 42
Windansea, 81
wineries, 27
Wreck Alley, 70, 141, 144